ALSO BY DOUG HENSCH

Positively Resilient
Re-Thinking Humility

Re-Thinking Curiosity

How to Lead When You Don't Have
All the Answers

Doug Hensch

Published by DRH Media

Copyright © 2024 Doug Hensch

ALL RIGHTS RESERVED

No part of this book may be translated, used, or reproduced in any form or by any means, in whole or in part, electronic or mechanical, including photocopying, recording, taping, or by any information storage or retrieval system without express written permission from the author or the publisher, except for the use in brief quotations within critical articles and reviews.

(DRHleadership.com)

Limits of Liability and Disclaimer of Warranty:

The authors and/or publisher shall not be liable for your misuse of this material. The contents are strictly for informational and educational purposes only.

Warning—Disclaimer:

The purpose of this book is to educate and entertain. The authors and/or publisher do not guarantee that anyone following these techniques, suggestions, tips, ideas, or strategies will become successful. The author and/or publisher shall have neither liability nor responsibility to anyone with respect to any loss or damage caused, or alleged to be caused, directly or indirectly by the information contained in this book. Further, readers should be aware that Internet websites listed in this work may have changed or disappeared between when this work was written and when it is read.

ISBN: 978-1-7365682-1-7

To Tammy
My model for curiosity and leadership.

Contents

Introduction – How did we get here? 1

Chapter 1 – Why is leading others so difficult? 5

Chapter 2 – Why doesn't the old way work? 19

Chapter 3 – What is the solution? 31

Chapter 4 – What makes curiosity so important? 39

Chapter 5 – Who can show me the way? 51

Chapter 6 – What else can I do? 61

Chapter 7 – What are the risks of having
    too much curiosity? 77

Chapter 8 – How can I encourage a culture
    of curiosity in my organization? 85

Conclusion 97

Acknowledgments 101

Sources 105

Introduction
How did we get here?

"The day that I don't learn something is the day that I die," my dad said to me when I was a kid. I don't fully remember the moment, only that I was probably complaining about some homework assigned in high school and he wasn't having any of it. His statement caught me by surprise. I had to pause and think about it. *What was he trying to tell me? What was I missing? How was his learning (and dying) relevant to me?*

My dad always had a book ready to be devoured. He would often come home from work, say "Hello" to everyone, and retreat to his chair and open whatever he was reading at the time. Sometimes, I would see him take out a yellow highlighter and start marking up pages. I admired the neat, almost perfectly straight lines he would draw. His handwriting was impeccable (most likely from years of producing drawings of the various blueprints for the machines, buildings, and other things that civil engineers design).

Another saying from my dad that landed firmly and planted itself in my memory: "People can take all your money and possessions away from you, but they can never take away your education." OK, this one made sense right away. He shared it with me when I was deciding where to go to college. The message: *Hey, it's great that you might want to play football in college ... but your real objective is*

Re-Thinking Curiosity

to get the best education possible. In short, he taught me the value of curiosity and its importance in developing a lifelong desire to learn.

My mom liked to read as well—just not as much as my dad. She exercised her curiosity in other ways. She asked my sisters and me about our days, what our friends were up to, and she didn't hesitate to snuggle up next to me while I was watching a documentary—the only exception being when I was engrossed in a World War II or Vietnam documentary, because she just didn't have the stomach for the violence.

Mom's fostering my curiosity didn't stop there. Just about every Christmas and every birthday, I received a book from her. Mom paid attention to what piqued my curiosity, and she fed it. I could bury my head in a good book even as a child. So, while she may not have enjoyed watching grainy footage of bombs dropping from B-17s, she didn't hesitate to get me a book on the subject.

I was (and still am) an incredibly lucky person. My parents modeled curiosity and they didn't shy away from answering my questions. They made every effort to help me help myself through learning and curiosity. For this, and many other reasons, I am eternally grateful.

***

You may be asking, "Why does the world need yet another book on leadership?" It's a valid question, since a recent search of Amazon.com for "leadership books" yielded over 60,000 results! Some of the top results came from amazing thought leaders, such as Admiral William McRaven, Brené Brown, Stephen Covey, and Daniel Coyle. I embarked on this journey because so much has been written on leadership, but very little on curiosity's relationship to it.

Doug Hensch

In 2009, I was introduced to Dr. Todd Kashdan, professor of psychology at George Mason University in Fairfax, Virginia. We met shortly after he published *Curious?: Discover the Missing Ingredient to a Fulfilling Life*. It is still *the* book to read if you want to understand this "hidden" strength. I was curious before I read it. I might be more curious now. What I have come to realize is that curiosity is a strength that I could apply to various domains of my life.

It wasn't just about learning about subjects that already interested me. It was also about directing my attention outside of these comfortable little buckets of content. I began to see curiosity as an ingredient to success at work and home. Being curious caused me to pause and think before deciding or acting. It opened up new possibilities and shut the door on others.

Pausing is something we do as coaches, too. We're taught to give our clients space to think for themselves, to help them help themselves. And we're taught to help our clients through the art and science of asking questions. It is absolutely exhilarating to watch a client transform. At the same time, it's not because I am some incredibly intelligent purveyor of wisdom. My approach centers around being curious. Over several thousand hours of coaching I came to the realization that while Kashdan's book was amazing, the word on curiosity was still not getting to enough leaders.

As you read on, ponder the questions that start each chapter. Feel free to jump around and experiment with what you learn or relearn. Discuss it with your team and run some experiments. Be skeptical. Be curious.

Re-Thinking Curiosity

Chapter 1
Why is leading others so difficult?

"The price of greatness is responsibility."—Winston Churchill

On rare occasions, my dad would get a call on our landline phone saying that a water main had burst, and he would leave to make sure that it was fixed properly and in a timely fashion. On most occasions, when Dad came home from work, he was home—physically and mentally. Not only was he present for dinner, he coached our Little League teams, he came to school concerts, and he was ready to help out on science projects. (To this day, I still remember how a parallel circuit works. Thanks, Dad!)

When he was at work, he had a modest office as the Vice President of Engineering. His days were filled with meetings in conference rooms, helping his engineers solve complex problems, looking over architectural designs and checking budget calculations. At most, he had an advanced Texas Instruments calculator to help with some of the more complex calculations. He didn't have a desktop computer at work until the late 1980s.

Around 1993, Dad brought home a laptop computer. Within a few years, he had a Nextel Motorola i1000 clipped on his belt. Now,

Dad could work on spreadsheets, presentations, job descriptions, email, and just about anything else from home. Dad was officially connected to work even when he wasn't at the office.

Dad seemed to love his work, and the laptop and phone came into his life when his kids were older, so there didn't seem to be a big impact on his personal life. Email and text messaging were in their infancy, so being home hadn't changed much for him or for us.

"Change is inevitable. Growth is optional."—John C. Maxwell

Fast-forward to 2024, and many things have changed in the past twenty or more years. I will not say that my dad's job as Vice President of Engineering was easy. He dealt with performance issues, poor hiring decisions, unreliable vendors, overconfident consultants, long hours, and tense union negotiations. Something has changed, however. Or should I say, things have changed? A short list of changes in our economy, culture, and workforce that make leadership more challenging include:

1. Accelerated change
2. Measuring employee engagement
3. Remote work management
4. Managing diversity & inclusion
5. Pressure to innovate
6. Talent retention & development
7. Effective communication

Doug Hensch

Today's leaders are balancing more than ever. What's missing? Family, health, changing priorities and more!

1. Accelerated change

Change in all its forms has been around since humans first set foot on our planet. Before the advent and dissemination of technologies like the printing press, automobile, airplane, and internet, it took decades for new discoveries and technologies to make their way across a single country. *New York Times* bestselling author and leadership researcher Liz Wiseman writes that while change has always been present, the pace of change is only increasing. Just several decades ago, it was estimated that approximately 10 percent of all knowledge across industries became outdated year over year. As recently as 2005, that number had jumped to 15 percent. Other studies suggest that in high-tech industries this number may be as high as 30 percent!

In addition, science is pumping out new discoveries and technologies at a much faster rate. So, new information is flowing in faster, and leaders therefore must keep up with all of this change at the same time, given that much of the information is outdated quickly. It used to be that experience and longevity were at least part of the criteria for selecting leaders. This is still true, but experience is clearly less valuable than it once was. Google may not give me a precise answer to my problem, but it can point me in the right direction. Chat GPT may not yet be 100 percent accurate, but it can help me get a great start to frame my issue and offer solutions which are surprisingly creative, insightful, and thoughtful. Therefore, the pressure to change and change quickly is immense.

2. Measuring employee engagement

In my first eight years of work, I had five different jobs. Some of that was by design, as this is the exploration phase of one's career where I decided to move to something more interesting and lucrative. But some of it was out of my hands—in one case, the company I was working for filed for bankruptcy. Moving around that much was risky. Friends and family constantly told me that I was going to be seen as a "job-hopper," implying that my supposed lack of loyalty might hurt me or short-circuit my career at some point.

They were right, to some extent. The prevailing wisdom at the time (and now to some extent) was that you should stay with a company for a couple of years to demonstrate a sense of loyalty and competence. Leaders embraced this belief and were more likely to have an employee base that was simply thankful to have a job.

In the early 2000s, however, this reality began to change. Companies began looking at employee engagement with the goal of reducing turnover and increasing productivity and profits. Gallup defines this as "the involvement and enthusiasm of employees in their work and workplace." The idea being that an engaged employee is better at solving problems, coming up with innovative ideas, and (here's one that employers really love!) putting in extra discretionary effort. In short, they work harder and make the organization more successful.

Based on their extensive research in this area, Gallup also asserts that only 32% of all US workers (23% worldwide) are considered "engaged." Their Q12 survey claims to identify the sources of disengagement and helps in getting everyone on board.

"I don't go to work hoping that I'm going to be engaged today," said Adam Grant, an organizational psychologist in the University of Pennsylvania's prestigious Wharton School, author of numerous bestselling books and host of the fascinating podcast ReThinking. He goes on to say that managers and companies are "obsessed" with engagement. He's not a fan of measuring engagement, because it doesn't take into account employees who are workaholics or those whose work-life balance is out of whack.

Ever since there have been leaders, there have been followers. The best leaders are constantly thinking about ways to motivate, reward, recognize, and develop talent in their organizations. However, attempts to measure employee engagement and satisfaction can sometimes backfire. Things like survey fatigue, fear of retribution for negative comments, and the nuanced nature of individuals make measurement of employee engagement extremely difficult to act upon in any meaningful way.

3. Remote work management

"Where will we put all the boxes and papers?" a CEO was heard saying several years ago at a startup when he realized that we were trying to convince him to let our office space lease run out as a cost-cutting measure. He had come out of retirement to lead this company, and his understanding of the technology that makes remote work possible was limited. He was worried that we just couldn't get our work done if we weren't in the office every day. Google Docs, Microsoft OneDrive, Zoom, and other tools didn't make him feel any more comfortable.

Today's leaders know that it is more than possible for employees to check off their to-do lists, collaborate electronically, and overcome challenges, all while working from a home office (even if it is the living room couch). COVID-19 accelerated our ability to be much more effective from remote locations, and now many offices are occupied by a fraction of the people that were there pre-COVID.

Now, managers don't always have the ability to walk over to someone's cube and ask a question. Meetings consist of looking at small videos of team members (assuming they turn their cameras on). And don't forget about the amount of cash being spent on office space that was recently renovated. Large numbers of employees have figured out that commuting cuts into family time, costs more in fuel, and is simply less convenient.

So, this leads us to some important questions. How do we get people back to the office? If we tell them to come back, will they just leave to work for someone else? If they do come back, how many days a week should they work from the office? Which days? If we just go 100% remote, what are the long-term effects on employee mental health, innovation, loyalty, and teamwork? Ian Leslie, author of *Curious*, refers to these as "mysteries" because they may not be solvable. "Puzzles," on the other hand, are what we're used to—challenges that have an answer. Getting comfortable with mysteries is now the norm.

4. Managing diversity and inclusion

I am 100 percent in favor of efforts to bring more diversity and inclusion to our organizations. There are numerous studies which indicate higher levels of innovation and better decision-making from diverse groups versus homogeneous groups. A 2017 study by McKinsey of more than 1,000 companies in twelve countries showed that higher levels of diversity led to both short-term profitability and long-term value creation. Another study of over 1,000 leading firms across multiple countries and two dozen industries discovered that gender diversity relates to more productive companies when diversity is widely accepted. And yet another study of more than 1,700 companies found a positive correlation between diversity and innovation that led to greater revenue. In short, there is legitimate research that suggests having a diverse workforce can improve your bottom line.

Set that aside for a moment. Fostering a workforce that better represents society is also simply a good thing to do. As a Partner (a white male in his mid-50s) at a large consulting firm once said to me, "When we go into a potential client's office to pitch for business, we have a much better chance of winning if we look like them. This firm pretty much looked like me when I first started. I am so proud that we have hired thousands of people that are very different from me."

And don't forget the concept of neurodiversity. People with autism spectrum disorder, for instance, are hardworking, focused, and gritty when in the right roles. The challenge is twofold here. First, hiring practices must change to allow for people not comfortable with the traditional interview process. Second, managers might have to allow these workers to wear headphones and skip social functions.

While the research points to better decision-making, outcomes, and innovation with greater diversity and inclusion, it also tells us that it's not easy. We can expect higher rates of disagreement, conflict, and personality issues. It takes time for more diverse teams to gel, and it can be uncomfortable.

My reason for pointing this out is not to critique, advise, or admonish. I mention it because the preceding generation of leaders didn't usually have to factor this into their personnel decisions or management operating style. In the famous words of the fictional Premier League coach, Ted Lasso, "All people are different people."

5. Pressure to innovate

Coming up with new ideas is easy for some people. Let's do a quick exercise. First, find an ordinary household item or something in your office that has a specific use like a paper clip, a spoon, or a pair of scissors. Now, think of at least 15 different uses for it. Here is an example of getting creative with a paper clip:

1. Holding several pieces of paper together
2. SIM card ejector for your phone
3. Cleaning between keys on your laptop
4. Scratching a really small itch with one of the tips
5. Popping a blister on your big toe from your new running shoes
6. Makeshift fishing hook
7. Resetting an electronic device that has one of those impossibly tiny holes
8. A key ring
9. A zipper pull
10. Opening an envelope

11. A really ugly earring
12. Cleaning dishwashing liquid spout
13. Money holder
14. String a bunch together to make a chain
15. A bookmark

If you gravitated toward this exercise, you probably have a preference for ideation (i.e., coming up with lots of ideas). Some people have more of a preference for clarifying the problem. They ask lots of questions and are determined to uncover the data that makes things clearer. Others like taking all these ideas and evaluating them. They may also get energy from building on existing ideas to make improvements, while others are all about getting things done. People who use the Nike motto "Just do it!" can get frustrated with lots of new ideas. They just want to get started!

In fact, people with each of these individual preferences can get frustrated with those with different preferences for solving complex problems. And, if you are constantly solving problems or charged with coming up with new ideas, this can make for a fair amount of personality conflict within your team. Anil doesn't like it when Susan rushes to a solution. Maria gets frustrated hearing about all of Joel's new ideas when the team is already behind schedule. And, so it goes.

Getting teams to work the right problem, come up with creative, practical ideas, develop these ideas into something that works, and then implement them is a tall task. The constant pressure to do so while most of your team works from home can be daunting, to say the least. Flexible work options (work-life balance), growth opportunities, meaningful work, and work culture are more important than salary for many people.

6. Talent retention and development

In the late 1990s, the economy was cooking. The internet boom had begun. GDP in the United States averaged growth of 4.5% per year by the end of the decade. Times were good for many Americans and companies. We even had a federal budget surplus. During this period, I worked for several wireless telecommunications companies, and growth was amazing at each company. This is when many people were buying mobile phones for the first time. Consequently, the telecom companies were investing heavily in advertising and infrastructure.

Employees were paying attention to the spending and the skyrocketing stock prices. And, they weren't to be left behind. In 1998, the prestigious consulting firm McKinsey & Company published a report based on several years of research saying there would be a "war for talent."

People were now free agents and were encouraged to offer their services to the highest bidder. We recently saw this up close from 2020 to 2022, when my clients would routinely tell me that they were losing their best people to 20% or 30% pay increases from other companies. Since annual pay increases typically hover in the 3–5% range for even the highest-performing employees, my clients couldn't match these offers. Gone are the days of employees working 30 years for one company. The "war for talent" is intense. It requires leaders to not just attract, but also retain and develop top talent. While some may say this has always been the responsibility of leadership, it has been taken to a new level.

7. Effective communication

You want to announce a new initiative that you and your leadership team have been cooking up for months. You and your team have spent countless hours brainstorming, planning, arguing, compromising, and discussing this plan. You're excited about the plan's prospects, and your team is excited as well. So, what to do next? You've got to communicate this detailed plan in a way that gets all or most of your organization motivated to implement it successfully.

In a pre-COVID world you might have just set up a town hall meeting in the auditorium and had your leaders each present a part of the plan to demonstrate that it was a collaborative effort and that it's going to take a coordinated effort to make this work. In today's world, an in-person town hall meeting might have a smattering of attendees with so many employees working from home. So, you decide to broadcast this over Zoom, Webex, or Microsoft Teams.

Half of those attending are multitasking. Another proportion have Zoom open and are technically attending, but they shut the sound off and are doing "work." You get the picture ...

Prior to the digital age, we either called someone on their desk phone or walked over to their office. Doing this made room for small talk, asking questions and getting a deeper understanding of how someone thought about an issue. Tone of voice, pitch, pace, and body language supplement the words we choose to convey and give them more meaning. Texts and emails are a poor substitute for an in-person meeting or a phone call.

There are generational differences, as well. When MIT psychologist Sherry Turkle asked her students why they weren't showing up for her office hours, the typical response was that it was just easier to text or email. I text and email all the time. It's just not the default form of communication for some of the reasons mentioned above. However, trying to call someone who really prefers texting can actually make it more difficult to communicate with this person when you go against their preferences.

Moreover, we have so many options for communicating with people that it's difficult for those sharing a message and those receiving it to know where to find information and which tool is the best for the situation at hand. People on the receiving end often have different preferences from their leaders, and this also makes it more difficult to lead today.

"Becoming a leader is synonymous with becoming yourself. It is precisely that simple and it is also that difficult."
—Warren Bennis

Okay, let's just admit that leading others is hard. It was hard 30 years ago, 100 years ago, and it's difficult today. For most of us, the natural inclination is to tell people what to do. We all have some level of a desire to control. Unfortunately, in most situations, this doesn't work as well as it used to. Today's employees expect a voice in important decisions, like how many days they are required to be in the office. Employees want to find more meaning in their work. Working for an organization whose greatest accomplishment is "twelve straight quarters of double-digit growth" doesn't get them excited.

We've simply got to find a new way to motivate, challenge, and include others to bring out the full power and engagement of today's workforce. It's not easy, and it requires hard work and experimentation. Curiosity unleashes the talent in others and takes the full burden of performance, innovation, and problem-solving and distributes it from the top floor to the bottom floor. In the next few chapters, we'll talk about what it means to be curious, how it can benefit you (professionally and personally!), what can get in the way of being curious, and some specific ways to add it to your leadership toolkit.

Chapter 2
Why doesn't the old way work?

"The old model of leadership was about control. The new model of leadership is about collaboration."—Ken Blanchard

Gail Fisher served in the United States Army National Guard and Army Reserve for a combined 33 years. The pressure to execute in the military and in business can be immense for some leaders. With that pressure comes the strong desire to simply tell people what to do. And if telling doesn't feel super comfortable (as it didn't for Gail), some leaders resort to being passive-aggressive.

When Gail felt the pressure to just get things done, she sometimes turned away from her curiosity and turned toward just telling people what to do, but in a way that felt like she was giving them a say. "To my regret, I have often set up situations where my subordinates found it easier to go along with my opinion," she told me. "I tend to be very forceful—even too aggressive sometimes. Like a little steamroller, when time is short and the stakes are high. This can serve to intimidate my subordinates who are not inclined to be so forceful. And then I am surprised that they are reluctant to engage with me and share their ideas," she said with a dose of humility and sarcasm.

Re-Thinking Curiosity

***

No leader is perfect. We all make mistakes. Great leaders, however, access their humility, admit their shortcomings, and decide to learn from them. Fisher shared her mistakes so others could learn. Her humility enabled her to be curious and make corrections.

Fisher is naturally curious. When she disagrees with her team, she often changes her mind after speaking. So, what happens when she becomes more "aggressive"? She sees it as simply being human. As a leader, she has a need to be heard, to be right, and to exercise some level of control. That's one of the reasons it's so difficult to lead from a place of curiosity. It requires humility and vulnerability. You're opening yourself up to the opinions, judgments, and viewpoints of others.

"Inclusive leadership is not a destination. It's a journey that requires humility, curiosity, and courage."—Thais Compoint

One framework that I have shared with a number of clients helps explain why "telling" can be ineffective. It comes from the work of psychologists Edward Deci and Richard Ryan in the 1980s. Unlike many other psychological theories, this one has stood the test of time. Deci and Ryan set out to gain a better understanding of human motivation. What they discovered is critical for today's leaders.

Self-Determination Theory (SDT) is made up of three components. It suggests that humans have three innate psychological needs. When these needs are met, individuals experience optimal growth, well-being, and motivation. When they are not met, employees experience lower motivation, put less energy into their work, and are probably less innovative and creative with the challenges they face.

Autonomy **Competence** **Relatedness**

True motivation requires leaders to give employees a sense of autonomy, lots of feedback to pursue competence, and the feeling that they are a part of something larger than themselves and connected to their colleagues.

1. Autonomy

When my kids were younger and I was a single dad, I was constantly looking for ways to build their sense of confidence and self-efficacy. I wanted them to have the ability to face the challenges that life throws at us all while pursuing meaningful goals. It wasn't easy, because I didn't want to see them make mistakes that could harm them or for them to get overly discouraged.

One summer, I found myself in a bind. I had to deliver an on-site workshop for a client that was about thirty minutes from my house, and I couldn't find someone to watch my kids. The boys were nine and ten at the time. Before I left for the day, I gave them very specific instructions about answering the door ("Do NOT answer the door!" I must have said about 50 times.) and asked them to call me if there was an emergency. That was it.

I was a bit of a wreck facilitating that day, wondering if I had made a colossal mistake. *Was I being reckless? Were they too young to be left alone that long?* I kept checking my phone, and I let my clients know my situation in case I looked distracted (which I was!).

When the workshop was over, I raced home, disregarding those white signs with black letters and numbers that say "speed limit." As soon as I pulled into the driveway, my youngest son (Zach) flung open the front door and came running down the stairs three steps at a time. He had the biggest smile on his face, and before I could say "Hello" and bombard him with questions about what he did that day, he launched into a very enthusiastic soliloquy. He began telling me about how he took the garbage out, made his bed, cleaned up the kitchen, and mowed the front yard. The smile on his face and the joy in his words said it all: *Dad, I did this all on my own, and I'm really proud of what I did!*

It was a fairly dramatic shift from the way our house normally operated, where I had to tell my kids to do all these things. I paused and tried to understand what had just happened. My nine-year-old was exercising his autonomy.

Your employees don't want to be micromanaged. They don't want to be told exactly what time they have to be at their desk, exactly how to create a PowerPoint presentation, or exactly how to finish a task. They are more likely to thrive when they have *some* level of autonomy about how to do their job. If you want to demotivate someone, treat them like they are nine years old and tell them exactly how to behave day in and day out.

2. Competence

When introducing the concept of competence to clients, I like to say that no one wakes up in the morning and says, "I can't wait to suck, today!" People want to be good at what they do even if they don't love it.

According to Deci and Ryan's research, there is a need to feel *effective* and *capable* in all of us. I believe that we may see this in adults more than children. Think about the last time you missed a deadline, didn't create a plan that accounted for some major issues, or gave a wrong answer in a meeting with your peers. How did that feel? I'm guessing you said, "Not good." At its best, it's a little embarrassing. At its worst, you may feel that your paycheck is at risk.

Joe Valerio was drafted in the second round of the National Football League (NFL) amateur draft by the Kansas City Chiefs in 1991. The six-foot-five, three-hundred-pound offensive lineman came out of the University of Pennsylvania (an Ivy League school that stresses academics over athletics) and he had to compete with bigger, faster young men from Alabama, Notre Dame, USC, and other powerhouse schools that offered scholarships and other perks that made it much easier to focus on football.

Still, Valerio had a productive career with the Chiefs and, at one time, was the career leader for offensive touchdowns by an interior lineman. After five seasons in the NFL, Valerio packed his bags and decided it was time to use his Ivy League degree as he moved back east to his hometown of Philadelphia. He took some time off to enjoy his newborn triplets and identify a career path that would use his head for solving problems rather than mashing it into other three-hundred-pound men.

He settled on the field of insurance brokerage and was hired for an entry-level position. About six months into his tenure with his new employer, we caught up over the phone. "So, how is life in your new job? How are you doing?" I asked him. Joe replied, "Buddy, I have no idea."

For the next couple of minutes, we talked about how every play that he was in on the field (both practices and games) was filmed … and watched over and over and over. "Valerio, you're sitting on your heels. You're telling our opponent it's a pass play!" he might hear from one coach. "Hey, 73 (Joe's number with the Chiefs), nice zone block," another coach might say. What Joe told me was that his initial foray into the white-collar world was frustrating. He really didn't know how he was doing. He was used to getting feedback—lots of it. How can you tell how you're performing if no one is telling you?

Managers back then (and many now) just didn't like to give feedback. Standard procedure at many companies was (and still is!) to give a performance review once a year. This is how they determined who got a raise, how much that raise was, and if there was a bonus to be awarded. Receiving feedback is essential for building competence. Our lens on our own skills and talents is often skewed.

I'm not one for using a lot of sports analogies as they don't always translate to the corporate world. With that being said, football, volleyball, softball and basketball coaches know that constant feedback is essential. And, it doesn't need to flow in one direction. Later, we'll talk about how to be curious in service of the people on your team and how to use it to improve your own competence.

3. Relatedness

Steve Jobs wasn't the most friendly, likable, compassionate leader. He denied stock grants to longtime employees, micromanaged numerous projects, publicly chastised engineers, and was quick to fire an employee he perceived to be underperforming. Despite this, his product innovations are on display throughout our society. iPads, iPhones, Apple TVs, and MacBooks are in just about every home in America and around the world. Almost all his greatest accomplishments, however, came after he learned some lessons from Ed Catmull at Pixar.

In 1986, Jobs made an investment in what was then a little-known company that eventually became Pixar. He was intrigued by co-founder Catmull's goal of creating movies solely from computer-generated imagery (CGI). With his investment, he made himself CEO. Catmull quickly noticed that Jobs' presence at content review meetings was killing the psychologically safe environment Catmull had worked so hard to build. People were not just afraid to speak up, they were afraid to show up. Jobs would attend these reviews with lists of changes he wanted to see and then bluntly state his opinions. If you've ever worked with creative people, you know there is some art and science to giving feedback in this arena. After several sessions, Catmull made a big decision—Jobs was asked not to attend these meetings. Then, Pixar cranked out one hit after another.

Over time, Jobs realized that people are not robots. They have feelings and emotions. And, they need to connect to other people. They need to connect to something larger than themselves. In short, people want to be loved and to love others. And, yes, we strive for this at work. We may think of "love" as meeting someone when we're 25 and spending the rest of our life with that person. Barbara Fredrickson's research on the subject shows that we experience love in what she refers to as "micro-moments"—small interactions where people demonstrate vulnerability, compassion, empathy, and understanding, for instance.

Jobs engaged in a bit of a correction when he rejoined Apple in the late 1990s. No, he didn't become an incredibly compassionate, caring leader. He did, however, spend more time thinking about the impact of his words and actions on others. As a coaching friend of mine likes to say, "He softened the sharp edges." With Apple having a market cap approaching three trillion dollars, the "new" Steve Jobs gets a lot of that credit even though he is no longer with us.

Jobs figured it out, and so can you. Today's employees don't just want great training, interesting work, opportunities for advancement, and big salaries. They want to know that they're a part of something bigger and that they're an important part of the team. Each person comes at this from different angles with different needs. Being curious allows us to gain a better understanding of those we work with, and that increases our chances of satisfying those needs.

"The only constant in life is change."—Heraclitus (535 BC)

Heraclitus gets a "high five" for that one. If he had also said, "And, it's going to get faster and faster!" I might buy him a beer. Fifty years ago, the turnover in knowledge across industries was about ten percent per year. This is sometimes referred to as the rate of decay of knowledge. A study in 2005 estimated that the rate had climbed to fifteen percent per year. A separate study puts that at 30 percent in high-tech fields. That was before artificial intelligence reached center stage ...

What does this mean for leaders? It's fairly simple. Your expertise and that of your "experts" is constantly expiring. Valuing knowledge was and is important in just about any industry. The difference is that experts today must stay on top of the changes in their fields like no other time in history.

In *Rookie Smarts—Why Learning Beats Knowing in the New Game of Work*, author Liz Wiseman argues that sprinkling more "rookies" throughout your organization provides several benefits, including questioning assumptions and being innovative. She defined a rookie as "someone who had never done that type of work and a veteran as someone who had previous experience with that type of work—both regardless of age." This is a very powerful concept and one that didn't get much attention several decades ago.

I had the great fortune of working for one of the most successful telecom companies of the last twenty years, Nextel Communications, which was eventually acquired by Sprint. Despite being much smaller than their entrenched competitors like AT&T and Verizon, Nextel routinely led the industry in two of the most important metrics: churn (the rate of turnover of customers) and ARPU (average revenue per user). It was also one of the only communications technologies to work at Ground Zero during the 9/11 terrorist attacks. In an industry not necessarily known for great customer service, it also ranked at the top for a number of years. Part of this success, I believe, came when CEO Tim Donahue made a change to his senior leadership team.

Rick Orchard was a veteran of the wireless industry and one who helped propel Nextel's sales team to new heights. Rick's team was great at bringing in new subscribers, and he was frustrated that customer care was not doing a better job of helping all these new customers and saving the ones that were dissatisfied. So, he began to complain to Tim. Eventually, Tim said, "OK, Rick, you think you know so much about it, how would you like to run customer care?" Rick the "rookie" used his curiosity to question assumptions, set higher standards, and turn the department around.

It was nothing short of a minor transformation, and just what the organization needed. Rick and his team started to question long-held assumptions, bring in some new ideas, and revitalize customer care. It wasn't easy, and the change didn't happen overnight. Rick came at it hard with his curiosity continuously asking, "Why are we doing this?" and eventually major changes took hold that propelled Nextel's customer care to be the best ranked by J.D. Power & Associates.

> **"In the digital age, leadership is less about command and control and more about inspiration and empowerment."**
> **—Brad Smith, former CEO, Intuit**

A changing workforce that wants more from their careers, fast-paced technological changes, and a reliance on knowledge are just some of the things that have changed. Today's leaders also must manage through:

- Lower levels of corporate loyalty
- Less trust and reliance on institutions
- Higher levels of narcissism
- Increased desire and ability to work remotely
- Greater competition from international companies
- Higher number of meetings
- Greater diversity in the workforce (a net positive for our society that brings with it some growing pains)

Re-Thinking Curiosity

If you still think it's not so hard to lead, consider a recent survey of over 16,000 managers in 23 countries. More managers than ever before are reporting they feel burnt out. It's gotten so bad that some recruiters are asking potential leaders how much they exercise!

According to the survey, intelligence still matters. The difference, however, is that all the interpersonal skills are rising in importance. Today's managers need to be coaches, therapists, mediators, and motivational gurus. Companies now value vulnerability, trust, and effective communication. Improved social skills are the key to coordination. Bringing different groups together to complete complex technical projects requires a leader to push, pull, cajole, decide, and collaborate, all at the right times.

In graduate school, I took a presentations course as an elective. The professor shared an oft-cited maxim before we started giving presentations to the class: *Tell them what you're gonna tell them. Then, tell them. And, finish by telling them what you told them.* Employees still benefit from being given some direction. This is how the average hierarchy works: The CEO shares the vision. Her Vice Presidents put plans together. Directors share the plans with Managers, and employees get it done.

In between, it's a lot messier. The CEO's vision usually doesn't see all the obstacles, risks, and issues that get in the way. The answer in a large majority of cases is to get curious. In fact, my experience is that most of the answers live on the front lines of your organization.

Gail Fisher figured it out with curiosity. So can you.

Chapter 3
What is the solution?

"Curiosity is the sweetest form of dissatisfaction."—Ian Leslie

One night after dinner, I decided to watch a little TV to help me relax after a long day at work. As we all know, watching TV is a passive experience that doesn't require taking notes, giving feedback, asking questions, or making difficult decisions. Yet it gives me a short time for my brain to take a much-needed break. Watching another *Seinfeld* episode for thirty minutes or laughing at the slapstick comedy of Will Ferrell in *Anchorman* relaxes me on most nights. On this night, however, I didn't opt for comedy. I stumbled upon a new five-part series from HBO called *The White House Plumbers,* which takes the audience from the Pentagon Papers all the way through the fateful decision to break into the Democratic National Committee headquarters at the Watergate Hotel ... *for a fourth time!*

After watching the first episode, I felt my curiosity begin to rise. All sorts of questions began randomly popping into my consciousness: *How did these guys get the funding for all these "dirty tricks"? Why were they so willing to break the law for someone else's gain? Who were these guys? Where did they come from?*

How did they get caught? What happened to each of them after Watergate? What was the role of Nixon and his closest aides?

At my fingertips were YouTube, Bing, Google, and Chat GPT. There was so much more to learn. And frankly, a fair amount of time to waste ...

It also turns out that the HBO series offered a riveting companion podcast that was available as each episode dropped. The podcast host interviewed the director and various cast members to help listeners understand where HBO took some creative license, why it inserted some made-up scenes, and how members of the production team identified locations for filming. One other person interviewed on the podcast was Garrett Graff, author of *Watergate—A New History.*

I quickly ordered Graff's book without reading the details, and it arrived in a couple of days. Much to my surprise, it was just over 800 pages. I dug in and somehow made the time to read enough each day to finish the book and give myself credit for probably knowing more (useless) information about Watergate than the average person. (If you're curious, there is some debate over whether the burglars broke into the Watergate Hotel three or four times.)

To some extent, my curiosity was satisfied as I closed the lengthy paperback for the last time and shoved it between two other books on the shelf. That itch was sufficiently scratched.

The first "flavor" of curiosity hits us just like that—an itch that needs to be scratched. We are exposed to information about something that draws us in *and* we are left wanting more in an effort to close the gap between what we know and what we'd like to know. (It's an instinctive process that we'll refer to as "natural" curiosity.) Depending on the intensity of the itch, we may go to Google for a quick search, YouTube to watch an expert about the subject, or Amazon to nuzzle up with a book on the subject.

Some experts promote this "gap theory of curiosity," which states that we evolved to be curious about the world by constantly trying to fill in gaps in our knowledge. This allowed us to ask, "How do we start a fire?" or "How might we get to the moon and back?" Questions beget answers that lead to more questions which, in many cases, lead to higher levels of achievement and goal attainment.

Some itches take a lifetime to scratch. (My interest in all things Watergate will most likely rear its head and draw me into various documentaries, articles, and books in the future.) Some lead to careers. Some lead to hobbies, and some lead to obsessions that can squeeze out family time, exercise, and other healthy endeavors. We'll talk about the downsides of too much curiosity later.

This first flavor is one most of us know all too well from our earliest days. Those itches led to questions, learning, and growing. Leaders, however, don't have as much free time as children. As a result, they may not be able to pursue as much as they would like. In fact, today's leaders routinely work over 60 hours per week and may not even be aware of their need to scratch an itch or feel they have the time to pursue their personal interests.

Re-Thinking Curiosity

CURIOSITY FLAVOR #1:
It's like scratching an itch

The second flavor is less like an itch that needs scratching and more like a dial that you control. You don't feel an "urge" to learn more about a subject. You *decide* to guide your attention with questions and inquiries in a specific direction. Usually, this is done to solve a problem or make a decision that is best for your organization. We'll refer to this flavor of curiosity as "directed." It's when we *choose* to focus on something rather than it calling our attention like an itch.

Effective leaders master the art and science of directing their attention and curiosity. They know when, where, and how to ask questions of their team, peers, and even customers to gain a better understanding of the situation. They read up on important issues, watch documentaries, or refine a Google search to learn more about what they think they need to know. In some cases, they know just to listen more than talk.

Doug Hensch

CURIOSITY FLAVOR #2:
Being able to direct your attention to what's important

"Curiosity is the most powerful thing you own."—James Cameron

Some more clues about the power of this word can be derived from its origins. The word "curious" comes from the Latin word "curiosus," which means "careful" or "inquisitive." And the word "curiosus" comes from the Latin word "cura," which means "care." The word "curious" was first used in the 14th century to mean "subtle, sophisticated." People who asked questions, showed interest in others, and embarked on continuous learning were seen in a positive light—it was a compliment to be called curious. In the late 14th century, it came closer to today's definition and meant "eager to know, inquisitive, desirous of seeing."

So, how does the word's origin help us understand it in the context of being an effective leader? First, an effective leader is often both "careful" and "inquisitive." She is *careful* not to plow through a decision or complex challenge, knowing that her current base of knowledge may not be sufficient. Her humility allows her curiosity to engage as she demonstrates a level of *inquisitiveness* that helps her (and her team) share different points of view to understand the challenge from multiple perspectives.

When it comes to *caring*, the effective leader shows his support for a beneficial solution to a problem by asking questions, allowing others to express their thoughts, and creating a culture that *cares* enough for all to be heard and understood. The effective leader knows that his power to make things happen most often lies beyond his current understanding. This power ultimately comes from the strength of his team members and their ability to engage.

"You can tell whether a man is clever by his answers. You can tell whether a man is wise by his questions."—Naguib Mahfouz

Today's experts share multiple, complementary attributes. Todd Kashdan, Professor of Psychology at George Mason University, writes that curiosity is *not* "just about being attentive; it's about the quality of our attention." In other words, am I really curious about what someone is saying when my head is buried in my phone? Am I attentive and interested if I'm distracted by my thoughts? To be truly curious, we must offer our full attention to that which is before us. Easier said than done …

Kashdan also shares five characteristics of curiosity that help us understand how complex it is:

Intensity—Are you captivated by what is in front of you?
Frequency—How often do you focus your attention on something new and interesting?
Durability—Is your interest fleeting or does it last for hours, days, weeks ... years?
Breadth—How many topics do you explore? Or, is there only one subject that really holds your attention?
Depth—Are you willing to put in the time to learn more and more about a subject, striving to know it inside and out?

The VIA Institute on Character was founded with the intent of helping people take a strengths-based approach to their work and personal lives. Its free assessment has helped over 27 million people identify their character strengths. One of these strengths is curiosity, and its definition of curiosity is rich and comprehensive. The team at VIA says that curious individuals share two characteristics: "They are interested in exploring new ideas, activities and experiences, and they also have a strong desire to increase their own personal knowledge." (To take the free assessment, go to www.VIAcharacter.org.)

Mario Livio, internationally known astrophysicist and author of the incredibly interesting book *Why?* told me that he was curious about curiosity. It took him almost five years to write this book, with the goal of gaining a better understanding of this subject. In the book, he identifies two types of curiosity from the work of Jordan Litman. The first, "I-curiosity," refers to those times when gathering more information is pleasurable or intrinsically satisfying. The second is "D-curiosity," and it signifies the instances when there is a sense of uncertainty, and we are deprived of information.

Next, we will explore the ins and outs of curiosity as it relates to leadership. It's not always possible to follow your personal passions as you strive to meet corporate goals, solve complex problems, develop innovative solutions, and manage people. Curiosity is not the only tool leaders can use to get results. As with humility, however, a lack of curiosity is a recipe for disaster. In the coming pages, we'll explore its benefits, the hazards of too much curiosity, how to apply it to your leadership practices, the obstacles you might face when trying to be curious, and how to get more of it for yourself and your team.

Chapter 4
What makes curiosity so important?

"That which doesn't kill us makes us stronger."—Friedrich Nietzsche

This quote is so ingrained in our culture that when I ran a Google search to make sure that I was spelling "Nietzsche" correctly, the first result was the song "Stronger (What Doesn't Kill You)" by Kelly Clarkson. The chorus of this song begins with "What doesn't kill you makes you stronger." (Just be happy that you don't have to listen to me try to sing this.)

Here are some other lines in the song of interest:

- "Just me, myself and I"
- "You didn't think that I'd come back—I'd come back swinging."
- "What doesn't kill you makes a fighter."

While inspiring to many, these lyrics may encourage us to go it alone, "throw punches" at adversity and be "fighters." In many cases, a mindset like this can cause more harm than good. It keeps adversity in a place where it almost becomes part of our identity.

Re-Thinking Curiosity

The uncomfortable emotions associated with the experience stir within us, never examined as to their usefulness.

It's not just Clarkson who is promoting this idea that difficulty and trauma are good for us. A number of studies in the last twenty years have promoted the idea that post-traumatic stress growth (PTSG) is a real phenomenon and that it's even more common than post-traumatic stress disorder (PTSD). Both PTSG and PTSD are real. They happen in cases of war, assault, and other traumas that adversely affect people. In the case of PTSG, some of us see the world differently after trauma and we "grow." According to this theory, we take the difficult experience and *decide* to be more resilient in the face of adversity moving forward. In short, the theory goes, we become better versions of ourselves.

This concept of growing through pain has even seeped into our entertainment. Batman, Spider-Man, and Wonder Woman all faced incredible hardships and adversity on their way to superhero status. Seems fairly benign and maybe even true, right? According to the Harold W. Tribble Professor of Psychology at Wake Forest, Eranda Jayawickreme, the research may not necessarily support Nietzsche's statement. It's not the trauma or adversity that makes us stronger, it's how we leverage our curiosity.

Jayawickreme recommends using both primary and secondary control strategies. Primary control strategies involve actions that directly modify or change something in our environment. As we discussed earlier, human beings crave a sense of agency.

When we exert our autonomy, we shift our mood and experience to more pleasant emotions. Executives can hire employees, fire employees, raise prices, implement marketing strategies, and change compensation to influence their situations, to name a few.

More difficult situations require greater levels of creativity and curiosity. In the spring of 2020 when COVID was wreaking havoc on the economy, one firm I worked with decided to mandate 10% pay cuts at the highest levels of the organization with smaller cuts at lower levels. The leadership team didn't want to send thousands to the unemployment line, so they got curious and asked, "What can we do to avoid layoffs?" The approach built loyalty *and* saved cash, which helped them manage their way through a difficult economic period.

Secondary control strategies also require curiosity. In this case, curiosity is not directed outwardly to the environment. It's aimed inward. It's an exercise in understanding oneself better and building self-awareness. The spread of COVID and its effect on the larger society was out of the control of most humans. An appropriate secondary strategy might be asking ourselves, "How would I like to *react* to this?" Doing this helps us accept the reality of the situation. It provides us with a better sense of self and makes difficulty more manageable. Research also shows that secondary control strategies improve satisfaction with life, not just our emotional response. I like to ask my clients, "How do you feel, *right now*?" The answers, of course, vary and change from minute to minute. I then ask, "How satisfied are you with your life?" and it produces much more stable responses.

Re-Thinking Curiosity

Secondary control strategies help us look in the mirror and set expectations about how we would like to act when adversity hits. Research shows that being curious about how we would like to react improves emotional responses.

As leaders, we are often taught to focus on primary control strategies. We do this as a response to situations that affect our organizations, and this is perfectly acceptable. It feels good to exert your autonomy with the goal of changing the environment to improve the situation. Leading through difficulty is often where a great leader leaves her mark and creates a positive legacy. Trying to control the uncontrollable, however, leaves one feeling less than adequate. The research suggests that approaching difficulty with *both* primary *and* secondary strategies is the best way to proceed.

"Listening was the most important thing that I accomplished each day because it would build the foundation of leadership for years to come."—Satya Nadella

There is a reason why the saying "It's lonely at the top" has been around so long. We've spent a whole chapter talking about how difficult it is to lead today. (It wasn't easy in the past, either!) That difficulty comes with a price. Too often the price is a higher level of stress, low work-life balance, extended hours at the office (home or business), eating poorly during business travel, and little or no exercise. There are several ways that curiosity can help alleviate the stress of leadership.

Susan David, author of *Emotional Agility—Get Unstuck, Embrace Change, and Thrive in Work and Life,* has an interesting take on how we manage our emotions. She argues that instead of trying to avoid or replace uncomfortable emotions, we are better off in the long run by facing them. When she was a child, her father died and, naturally, she was devastated. At the urging of a compassionate teacher, she began writing about her emotions. She discovered that facing the emotions brought about by this tragedy helped her move *through* this difficult period.

David calls ignoring or avoiding uncomfortable feelings "bottling." Like a bottle of soda with a partially open top, these feelings eventually "leak" out and disrupt our lives, sometimes with behaviors that do not align with our values. One study showed that people who kept their emotions to themselves actually raised the blood pressure of those around them! As a leader, your team is watching your every move and feeling what you are keeping inside.

Instead, getting curious frees you to learn more about yourself and face these challenges. There are no good or bad emotions. Anger, embarrassment, anxiety, and fear (among others) are simply markers. They are telling us that we're not comfortable with the current situation and that we may need to take action or sit still. Simply asking yourself, "What are these emotions telling me?" helps you take more of an outside view and be more objective about your situation.

A number of studies have also shown that simply being curious can drive well-being higher.

- One study from 2013 showed that curiosity was one of the strengths that displayed a strong connection to eating healthier, leading an active life, and pursuing enjoyable activities.
- A study from 2021 examined a combination of people who experienced loss and those who did not. For those with the signature strength of curiosity, there were fewer incidences of depression. (Other strengths that were correlated with these results included hope, zest, gratitude, love, spirituality, prudence, and self-regulation.)
- A Greek study during COVID found curiosity was associated with higher well-being during quarantine.
- In 2014, a group of researchers determined that curiosity was positively associated with life satisfaction and positive affect.

Michael Chiock is not your average management consultant. I met him over a Zoom call in the depths of the COVID pandemic during a virtual workshop that I was co-facilitating for his firm, AlixPartners. His role in this training was to offer feedback to each group of participants after they had presented their case study findings. The participants were junior consultants, and this training prepared them to present to clients. Understandably, there were some nervous presenters that day.

I quickly discovered that Michael's advice was always spot-on, and he delivered each critique with humility. He usually posed a question or two to the groups he was speaking with to clarify why they had presented certain information and excluded others. The feedback wasn't biting. It was accurate and behavioral. Michael was honest *and* kind.

Fast-forward to the fall of 2022, and I had the great good fortune of meeting Michael in person when we were able to deliver the training in-person at a Boston hotel. After the training concluded one day that week, he asked me to join him and other Managing Directors (MDs) for dinner. I was flattered and curious about how this would go, as three MDs probably wanted to talk shop and most of it would go straight over my head! Michael and the other two MDs were incredibly gracious and curious, as well. They asked me about my company, what it was like to be an executive coach, and about my family. At the time, my youngest son (Zach) was completing his senior high school season of football, and the team was poised for the play-offs. I mentioned this and shared that I would be hopping on the earliest flight Friday to see Zach's game.

Six months later, we ran the training again, and as Michael and I shook hands, he immediately asked how Zach's season turned out. I was almost speechless because he remembered, and he cared enough to follow up. After spending another few days with Michael, I realized this wasn't a tactic or ploy to win me over. This is Michael. He's curious about other people in a genuine way.

During a discussion about this book, I asked Michael if he had ever been curious in a way that led to greater well-being and/or better physical health for him. About a month into COVID, when most of us were isolating and business travel ground to a halt, Michael's wife said she noticed that "something was off" with him and that "he needed to figure it out."

He decided to get curious and "trace his steps." That is, he wanted to figure out what had changed and how that was affecting him. "As I dissected it, I realized that I used to spend a large portion of my days by myself. A typical Monday morning had me taking an Uber to the airport to visit a client with my earbuds in. Then, I'm on a plane … with my earbuds in or reading a book. After that, it's another taxi ride by myself, listening to a book or a podcast," Michael told me. He continued with a typical consulting day that included some meals alone, workouts alone, and time in a hotel room by himself that all included a podcast, a book, or some other form of intellectual stimulation. Michael has a "thirst for learning" and had to find a way to get that time back.

The COVID lockdown had changed his routine, so he got a little creative. He began taking certain phone calls on walks, for instance. When the call was over, he would continue walking and listen to a podcast or an audio book. Problem solved.

Michael's curiosity (and that of his "brilliant" wife!) helped him help himself. It didn't take a ton of effort and he didn't get defensive with his wife's comment. He got curious.

Doug Hensch

"There is no better catalyst to success than curiosity."
—Michael Dell

This is all well and good. Curiosity is good for our physical and mental health as individuals. What does it mean for leaders and the success of their organizations? Here is a great lesson that may impact everyone reading this book.

The food we eat, the clothes we wear, and just about every product that is manufactured comes in contact with or is produced with man-made chemicals. In some cases, these chemicals are toxic, and a number of governmental agencies, including the Food and Drug Administration (FDA) and the Environmental Protection Agency (EPA), are focused on limiting the amount of harm these chemicals do.

Up until a few years ago, testing chemicals was limited to high doses with animals. The standard methodology was to test one chemical at a time. The cost in time (years) and money (millions) is significant to a country whose commerce has roughly 80,000 chemicals and produces almost 8,000 new chemicals a year. Consider the shirt you are wearing. One or more of the chemicals used to make the shirt may have been approved as safe for making contact with human skin. Eventually, your shirt will make its way to the garbage can and a landfill. The chemicals may leak into our water supply and be consumed by humans. Since the original intent for testing the chemical in the shirt was to see how it reacted with human skin, we have no way of knowing how it affects us if ingested. It is a daunting task to find out, to say the least.

Re-Thinking Curiosity

In 2006, Chris Austin was asked to lead a large toxicology program that was to be a joint effort between his organization (National Institutes of Health), EPA, and FDA. He and his team were tasked with coming up with a way to evaluate chemicals in a more efficient manner. This might just lead to solving the problem of the edible T-shirt...

Like many executives, he was charged with solving an important problem with a high degree of complexity. And, in most situations, Chris is the smartest person in the room.

He got his undergraduate degree in Biology from Princeton, then drove north and worked his way through Harvard Medical School. He is undoubtedly intelligent, educated, and well-trained. The problem was that Chris "knew literally nothing about toxicology" when he joined this project.

After several years of work, the team made headway on simplifying the testing of chemicals to the point where the EPA said it will eliminate the need for animals in the process. Chris credits his own curiosity and that of his team as the key ingredient not only in their success but in the speed with which they worked. Each member of the team had the humility and curiosity to admit what they didn't know and look to their peers for answers. "We spent hours upon hours asking each other questions that advanced our knowledge. We had to come at it with both humility and curiosity. This allowed us to learn much more rapidly than if we had worked in isolation within our own areas of expertise. We really relied on one another," Chris told me.

I have had the privilege of coaching several hundred leaders for over a decade. And, after several thousand hours of coaching, one thing is certain: being a leader can be incredibly stressful. When Chris Austin first heard that the EPA wanted to eliminate animal testing entirely by 2030 and that he was leading a project that was going to help make this happen, he had a knot in the pit of his stomach. He may have even said to himself, "How the heck am I going to make this happen?" The saying "It's lonely at the top" has some truth to it. And, therein lies one of the most common challenges: facing the belief that you are going at it alone.

As Chris Austin and his team demonstrated, curiosity helps leaders access important information from others. His project was virtually impossible without the input of experts from other disciplines. He demonstrated his intelligence and humility by sending the message that he didn't have all the answers and that he was open to being influenced.

"Much of what I stumbled into by following my curiosity and intuition turned out to be priceless later on."—Steve Jobs

In 2023, the DRH Group commissioned a study to ask employees how they viewed curiosity as it related to their own leaders. The first thing we did was to ask respondents to rank curiosity as it compared to nine other leadership traits: fairness, self-awareness, empathy, humility, kindness, creativity, optimism/hope, passion, and self-regulation. Curiosity was dead last. How come?

The answer may lie in an activity we often run at the beginning of our leadership workshops. We ask participants to share the first words that come to mind when thinking about great leadership. The results by a vast majority fall into one of two categories. First, we hear words that describe emotional intelligence. They include terms such as self-aware, calm, empathic, and collaborative. Second, we hear words that seem to refer to the older style of leadership where we looked for our leaders to be decisive, knowledgeable, and experienced. Being curious is just not top of mind. It's also something that, like humility, is difficult to see and measure.

Participants in our survey were also asked about the level of curiosity they saw in the "very best leader" they had worked with or observed. Almost 80% of the respondents rated these top leaders as being very curious. So, while curiosity may not be rated as high as self-awareness, empathy, creativity, and kindness, it is *necessary* for these characteristics to flourish. Without curiosity, it is virtually impossible to begin to understand another human being, evaluate alternatives from a problem-solving session, and even recognize our own motivations, biases, and tendencies.

Next, we'll explore how curiosity is used by a diverse group of leaders who are changing their organizations one question at a time.

Chapter 5
Who can show me the way?

"A good leader inspires people to have confidence in the leader; a great leader inspires people to have confidence in themselves."
—Eleanor Roosevelt

My initial conversations with coaching clients usually start with my asking, "So, what do you know about coaching?" I ask because I want to know how much detail to give about what coaching is and what coaching is not. In fact, my own answer to this before I started working with leaders was that coaching was what we saw in athletics—the coach tells the players what to do and how to do it. It turns out that the sports equivalent is very different from what effective coaching for leaders looks like. Executive coaches lead with questions and occasionally offer options for leaders to choose from for important decisions, problem-solving, and other issues they bring to the table.

What many think of as coaching (the football or basketball coach having all the knowledge and directing activity) is actually closer to what we refer to as "mentoring." Mentoring is a fantastic way to learn from someone who has been in your shoes and can offer real-world anecdotes and advice based on their own experiences. And, therein lies one of the shortcomings of mentoring. It is the mentor's life experience, not yours.

This chapter might feel a little like mentoring. It's focused on sharing the experiences of a handful of experienced, successful leaders who were kind enough to share their thoughts and recommendations. As you read along, see what is relevant to you and how you might apply these lessons in *your* context. If the lesson applies to you, adopt it into your leadership. Or, as a good friend of mine once told me when he was teaching me how to facilitate a workshop, "Doug, just make it your own."

***

Admiral John Richardson (Ret.) was the Chief of Naval Operations (CNO) of the United States Navy from 2015 to 2019. John led and served on teams that have been awarded the Presidential Unit Citation, the Joint Meritorious Unit Award, the Navy Unit Commendation, and the Navy "E" Ribbon. For his command of the USS *Honolulu*, he was awarded the Vice Admiral Stockdale Award. John is an extraordinary leader.

Even though he has been retired from the Navy for several years, John looks like he could run a marathon. He keeps his calendar busy, and he continues to be curious. When I reached out to him about my previous book on humility, he jumped at the chance to talk about this ancient, critical virtue. When I rolled the dice again for this book, John was no less enthusiastic, engaged, and ready to discuss his thoughts on this subject as it relates to leadership. John's enthusiasm was evident from the beginning of our first conversation when he said that curiosity "is the fruit of humility. It's super important. Things are always changing, and you have to continue to learn."

More specifically, when he was CNO and stationed in Washington, DC, he made regular visits to various installations with the goals of gauging progress on projects, holding leaders to standards, and helping them solve problems. When on-site, he made it a point to be curious with the teams he met to "make personal connections," which led to better problem-solving. When people feel cared for, heard, and understood, they're more willing to admit mistakes, share problems, and offer solutions. Being truly curious gets people talking. Being humble enough to hear whatever they have to say keeps them talking. He likes to say that leaders "honor" their teams when they seek their advice and wisdom.

When it comes to evaluating leadership talent, when he sees a leader asking questions and listening with humility, he knows he has an engaged leader. Asking deep, thought-provoking questions creates the conditions that can lead to a culture of excellence. John didn't just want to meet the standards and goals set out for him and his teams. He wanted to create a culture that was focused on achieving "best-ever performance." "How do you do that?" I asked. "Lots of curiosity!" he replied.

"Around here, we don't look backward for very long. We keep moving forward, opening up new doors and doing new things, because we're curious ... and curiosity keeps leading us down new paths."—Walt Disney

Re-Thinking Curiosity

Katherine Huh, Partner at PricewaterhouseCoopers (PwC), took Walt Disney's advice and developed a whole new line of business with her curiosity. And, it wasn't easy. Katherine is one of only two people of color that are Partners on the Financial Services team. Being curious and offering new ideas can be risky and leave leaders feeling vulnerable. Most spend a lot of energy proving how competent they are, not asking questions about things they don't know. Not Katherine.

Katherine and her team were working with various clients in the New York City metro area on a variety of real estate projects. She had listened to several senior Partners talk about how important it was for PwC employees to be entrepreneurial. So, Katherine activated her curiosity and started asking questions within the firm to see what might be possible. *Why don't we help our clients with site selection? What about construction project management? What if we helped them with space optimization, facilities management, and lease management?*

One thing led to another, and Katherine kept "poking around" to see which other firms offered all these services and why PwC didn't. It turns out that no one was asking these same questions. Katherine was on to something. When I asked her if she had experience with site selection, construction project management, and the other services, her response was, "No. I really had nothing to back it up except the fact that we had excellent relationships with our clients. They trusted us when we came to them saying that PwC had not done this exact work before."

Katherine led a few small test projects which eventually turned into revenue of approximately $20 million per year. She searched around within the firm for staff who had transferable skills and would bring their own curiosity to build the "muscles" to offer this to a wider set of clients in the future. She trusted her gut and her team. In fact, she pushed back on taking credit for this and said, "It was really the team that built this. They genuinely care for each other." Humility + Curiosity = Success

"Computers are useless. They only give you answers."
—Pablo Picasso

Of course, Mr. Picasso (who passed away in 1973) didn't get to witness the personal computer revolution, smartphones, or Chat GPT. Sumeet Sabharwal graduated from Cornell University with a degree in Electrical Engineering and Computer Science. You might think he would have a difference of opinion with the famous painter. Not so much.

Sumeet, the CEO of Netgain Technology, presides over an organization that is a multicloud managed services firm which provides secure and scalable IT-as-a-Service (ITaaS) for healthcare, financial services, and legal organizations. He values curiosity so much that it is now a part of the culture at Netgain. "I hire for it," he told me. "I am judging for curiosity right up front in the way I interview. And, the good candidates are the ones that have done their research that are always asking the non-obvious questions. It's that level of curiosity that plays to our advantage at numerous places."

Those non-obvious questions have helped Netgain turn issues into opportunities. One example that Sumeet shared had to do with a member of his staff. He said that he is "blessed" with a curious Vice President of Finance who drove over $5 million in annualized savings by asking questions about various expenses and how they could be reduced. This is a great example of making curiosity a core value where it becomes a part of the culture.

He tells his team that it's important to "be the last to speak." He encourages them to probe and "go deep" on issues. He sees conversation with the people on the front lines as critical to truly understanding issues and finding opportunities.

Be ready to learn from leaders who demonstrate humility and curiosity. Great leaders show us the way with their words and their actions. Pay attention to leaders who make others feel safe to be curious.

"The ability to observe without evaluating is the highest form of intelligence."—Jiddu Krishnamurti

Sometimes, we pass judgment on ourselves and others without recognizing that it's happening. We jump to conclusions at the speed of light, and our conscious minds just accept our point of view without challenging it. We all do it, and it's part of the human condition.

- I didn't get promoted because I haven't been here long enough.
- He interrupts me because he doesn't respect me.
- I'm too inexperienced to lead this project.
- The new analyst is not meeting deadlines because she's not motivated enough.

Kiera McCaffrey learned this the hard way. On her way up the ranks at a strategic communications and marketing firm based out of Alexandria, Virginia, Kiera had her eyes on a long-term business development opportunity with a key client. In her mind, she was a natural fit for the leadership role on this project. But when roles were assigned, the Partners left Kiera's name off the list.

"I just assumed that they didn't think I was fit for this. It must mean that I hadn't shown well in this area," she told me. Kiera was disappointed in herself. It wasn't that she thought those chosen by the Partners weren't a good fit. She was just surprised she didn't get a spot on the team. It was a real blow to her confidence. She added, "You know, I didn't really ask any questions. I just accepted their decision and my conclusions about the situation."

Several months went by, and Kiera joined one of the Partners for lunch. He asked her to take a senior leadership role on this same project. "Hey, I'd love to do it. At the same time, I'm kind of confused. You passed over me originally and it seemed like you didn't think I was ready for this," she told the Partner. "Where the heck did you ever get that idea? We were considering your workload, who would be best to kick this off and how you might come in later to lead," he replied.

In retrospect, Kiera wished that she'd recognized how quickly she had judged herself and the situation. A curious approach would have helped her see the "light at the end of the tunnel." The firm's leadership valued her and just assumed that she understood their rationale. So, for the several months before her lunch, she put her nose to the grindstone to "show them how great [she] was" and it took a toll on her—undeserved stress, a little extra anxiety, additional hours at the office, and a lower level of confidence. And, all she needed was a well-placed question: *Hey, Jack, I'm just curious. What was the process for selecting the lead on this project?*

"I am neither clever nor especially gifted. I am only very, very curious."—Albert Einstein

I can imagine Luis Viera saying something similar. I've known him for several years and I have been impressed by the results he gets and the culture he is building at Aleto, a small, growing consulting firm that supports federal government agencies and enterprises by providing facility support services and a wide range of solutions focused on real estate issues. The minute you meet Luis, you know he cares about his team.

When asked about how he used curiosity as a leader, I got a very matter-of-fact answer, "I use it every day." It was almost as if to say, "How can you even ask that? It's essential to how I lead."

Then, he began to recount a situation from the previous day where someone on his team called with their "hair on fire." There was a dispute with a client that involved miscommunication on both sides. By asking questions and keeping the goal in mind, Luis determined that they needed to identify a solution as quickly as possible, as the funds to complete the project needed to be spent in the closing months of the year. On top of that, by doing nothing, there was a health risk. They had to replace some equipment at the client's office before somebody got hurt.

With Luis' 20+ years of experience, the easy route would have been to simply suggest a path forward. He's been around the block more than once. As President of the firm, he knew there needed to be a solution in place quickly. Luis activated his humility and walked around to speak with various members of the team to get their perspectives. Instead of jumping to conclusions and giving directions, he asked questions and listened.

After spending a full hour speaking with four or five people, he came back to his office and started mapping out what he knew on a whiteboard. "It kind of looked like one of those scenes in a detective show where there are pictures, callouts, text, and red lines connecting images," he joked. Luis put aside all the emotions and baggage that had prevented a realistic solution from emerging. "What you don't know inevitably comes to haunt you," he said. "Getting curious as a leader reduces your risk and exposes solutions."

Luis Viera, Admiral Richardson, Katherine Huh, Sumeet Sabharwal, and Kiera McCaffrey are great examples of curious leaders. At the same time, they wielded their curiosity in a way that fit their situations for maximum benefit. Each would surely tell you that it wasn't always natural for them and that they made lots of mistakes. If you are of the old mindset where telling people what to do was your way of leading, consider taking small steps to shift your mindset. Experiment and learn.

Next, we're going to give you 25 different tips, tools, and ideas to help you bring more curiosity to your organization.

Chapter 6
What else can I do?

"Curiosity about the world and questioning of the status quo to open minds to alternative visions of the future are essential leadership skills. And they can be learned."
—Stewart D. Friedman

Several years ago, a senior executive in financial services reached out to me about coaching. Tim (a fictional name to protect the client's privacy) was performing at a high level. He was respected and in line for a promotion. "What is it that brings us together today?" I asked him after some brief small talk. Tim proceeded to tell me how well things were going for him and for the company. Then, he shared that there were a couple of relationships that were in need of repair and that he was not as motivated by the work as he used to be.

Our initial conversation went well enough that Tim hired me, and we began our work together. From the beginning, it was easy to see that Tim was intelligent, experienced, and caring. However, he was stuck. The relationships that were in trouble couldn't be fixed with his intellect. He had mastered his current role, and the joy of the challenge was missing.

Re-Thinking Curiosity

We talked about Tim bringing more curiosity to his work. Slowly he began to shift from being the "answer man" to the "guy with a lot of questions." He had always been a curious person. He loved to read books, watch documentaries, and go to museums away from work. At work, however, he was different. Tim was so focused on results that he had forgotten about process and the value of being curious. With a slight shift in his mindset (from "knowing" to "curious"), he improved his relationship with others and found new interest in his work. Instead of judging others and assuming he knew their motives, now he asked and listened. Instead of thinking that he knew the answers to complex challenges, he engaged others with questions and encouraged them to share their ideas.

In chapter 3 ("What is the solution?"), we talked about the definition of curiosity and the idea that there are "flavors" of curiosity. *Natural* curiosity seems to happen *to* us. We see or hear something that activates our interest, and we explore. We try to "scratch the itch" or satisfy a hunger within us for more information. Tim had plenty of natural curiosity, as mentioned above.

Unfortunately, leaders are not always confronted with challenges that are of interest to them. On any given day, you might be confronted with a variety of issues and situations that are not only outside of your areas of interest, but they are also difficult, complex, and frustrating. In these cases, *directed* curiosity is your best friend—when you choose to be mindful, present, and curious to meet the challenge. This is where Tim excelled, and so can you.

"Becoming is better than being. The fixed mindset can make you feel inferior or superior, but the growth mindset makes you feel like a constantly evolving work in progress."—Carol Dweck

So, can you become more curious? I was listening to a podcast the other day to answer this question. The host and the guest didn't think this was possible. They both argued that whether you are born with lots of curiosity or it's fostered by your parents or a great teacher, it's not something you can truly develop as an adult. I wasn't satisfied with this answer, so I looked a little further and attempted to find an analogous behavior. I discovered multiple articles citing the number of times a child laughs each day compared to the number of giggles coming from an adult. Have you heard that kids laugh about 300 times each day versus only 17 from adults? It turns out that this is an urban legend. Most likely, kids do laugh more than adults, but it's certainly not in the ratio of 300 to 17. For the kindergartener who is awake for 13 hours, she would need to laugh every 2.6 minutes! And most likely, adults can learn to laugh more.

As for asking questions, it is also difficult to find anything resembling peer-reviewed research that gives us a confident answer to how many questions are asked in a day by kids and by adults. Interestingly, the articles I did find have a similar ratio. Again, I think it's fair to say that kids tend to ask more questions than adults. *Why is the sky blue? Where do babies come from?* Many "experts" say that we drive curiosity out of kids by giving them tests that require the memorization of facts and figures instead of teaching and testing critical thinking. And many adults are afraid to ask questions for fear of looking incompetent. Again, I believe that adults can relearn the ability to bring a childlike curiosity to their work.

The tips and tools below are not from peer-reviewed research. They are, however, techniques and practices that have worked for my clients and those of my peers with positive results. I have witnessed a number of senior executives change their mindset and behavior to be more curious.

Menus can be intimidating. If I get chicken parm, will I regret it? Here's a menu with no regrets. We've compiled 25 tips, tools and tricks to help you weave more curiosity into your leadership approach.

"The important and difficult job is never to find the right answers. It is to find the right question. For there are few things as useless—if not dangerous—as the right answer to the wrong question."—Peter Drucker

Here are 25 tips for boosting your curiosity. Take them and make them your own by combining and adopting them as you see fit. The point is to put some effort into strengthening your curiosity muscle.

1. **Get bored**—That's right, the next time you instinctively reach for your phone when you're waiting to get on a plane or in line at the grocery, stop. Pay attention to what's going on around you. Practice asking yourself questions. *Why did the airline choose to board the plane this way? What's it like for the gate agents to deal with difficult customers? How much training does a cashier have to take before being able to run a checkout with no supervision?* Practice being in the moment and see what you notice and resist the temptation to get lost in your device.

2. **Imagine that everyone in the room is smarter than you**— You may not be the least bit arrogant. With enough experience, it's easy to think you have the "right" answers to many of the challenges you face. It's natural to have confidence in yourself; however, having the answers robs your team of the chance to grow. Make it a point to speak last after you or someone else brings up an issue. As soon as you share your point of view, others will line up behind you. Adopt the habit of speaking last and listening more.

3. **Stop asking for feedback**—"I keep asking my team for feedback, but all I get are blank stares or vague comments that

don't really help me," one client once told me. Most people are intimidated by power. On top of that, the word "feedback" has evolved into something that is almost exclusively negative. Instead, replace the word "feedback" with "advice." *I'd like to be more effective running our staff meetings. What advice do you have for me?* Several studies show that you will receive more input *and* it will be more actionable.

4. **Be a problem finder**—Alan Robinson, PhD, has been teaching and conducting research at the University of Massachusetts for several decades. In addition, he has built a successful consulting practice helping companies innovate more effectively. Alan has written over a dozen books on innovation, and one piece of advice that sticks out to me is that he trains employees to start looking for problems. *Why do I need to input this information twice? How can we onboard a client faster? What other vendors offer this product with better customer service?* It does not mean you have to take a pessimistic view of your organization. It means looking for issues and bringing your team in to solve them. Removing obstacles from the paths of your employees and customers scores you points and creates piles of goodwill.

5. **Put it on your calendar**—We all know that eating, sleeping, and exercising are important. Have you ever thought of taking time to just think? The famous psychology research team of Amos Tversky and Daniel Kahneman would take

two- to three-hour walks and just talk about problems they'd like to solve. You probably don't have two or three hours to carve out of your day, but do you have 15–20 minutes to take a walk and just think? Get away from your desk, try not to bring your phone, and pay attention to your surroundings. See what you notice. It's a great mindfulness exercise, and it also gives your brain a chance to incubate some of your more pressing, difficult issues.

6. **Adopt a growth mindset**—Do you believe that characteristics like creativity, intelligence, and empathy are immutable? Or do you think that people can improve their creativity, intelligence, and empathy? Psychologist Carol Dweck's research tells us that answering "Yes" to question number two is an indicator that you may have a "growth mindset," which also correlates to higher levels of resilience and curiosity. When we believe that we (and those around us) can improve our skills, we begin to ask questions. *Who can teach me? What might I do to improve? How can I set aside some time to develop this skill? How can I do my job better?*

7. **Beware of "Why"**—Getting to the root of an issue is usually the best path to a complete solution. Beginning your inquiry of another person (particularly when there are some uncomfortable emotions in the air) with "Why …?" is a little bit like a nuclear power plant. When everything is safe and secure, "Why" helps unlock root causes. When one or both parties

are feeling threatened or unsafe, asking "Why" forces the other person to defend their position instead of sharing their thought process, and risks an explosion. Replace "Why did you hire that vendor?" with something like "What was the process for selecting a vendor?" or "How did the team go about making this decision?" You'll get a readout of their process with little or no defensiveness.

8. **Strive for understanding**—Being wrong doesn't feel good. It feels worse when you think it might jeopardize your standing with your group and possibly lead to you losing your job. As a result, we often focus on proving that we're right. I believe there are only upsides to trying to understand those whom we disagree with, especially when it's hitting a nerve with us. Remember that understanding does not equal agreement. Recognizing the point of view of your "opponent" only helps you find common ground and potential solutions. The next time you disagree with someone, make your stated goal to understand the other person *before* you decide to state your case.

9. **Take mindfulness walks**—I'm a big proponent of the idea that sitting is the new smoking. We need to get up and move around more as a species. I do my best to get 10,000 steps a day, and I decided to meditate for a couple of minutes each morning once I learned of the benefits of mindfulness. Try combining the two. The next time you take a walk, try using

your five senses to practice some mindfulness. *What are you seeing with your eyes? What sounds can you identify? What physical sensations do you feel? How many things can you smell? What tastes are still lingering?* BONUS: Spend more time working on the senses that are NOT as strong to develop a more well-rounded approach to observing the world.

10. **Watch *MythBusters*—**That's right, watch a little TV. Maybe it's a documentary, a cooking contest, or a home improvement show. Pay attention to how they ask each other questions and solve problems. Get curious as if you were a part of the production and ask some open-ended questions about the challenges they face. *How are they going to do this? What scenes did they delete? How many people are involved in making this show?* And, if you do opt for *MythBusters*, don't be afraid to ask, "What can I do to love my job as much as these guys?"

11. **Practice the 5 Whys**—Surface-level answers fix surface-level problems. Leaders who ask great questions and persist when they get surface-level answers are more likely to get to the root cause of a problem. The process starts with a problem statement, and then the question "Why?" is asked. Each answer forms the basis of the next "Why?" question. This iterative questioning process helps to peel away the layers of symptoms, leading to the underlying cause. It's a simple yet powerful tool for troubleshooting, quality improvement, and problem-solving in various domains. (Keep in

mind, "Why" can still cause defensiveness in others. If you think everyone feels safe, use "Why." If some might get defensive, change your "Why" questions into "How" or "What" questions.)

12. **Go on an advice fast**—Depending on the nutrition theory you subscribe to, you may have attempted to fast for some period of time and had some success (or not!). I've tried it. It's not easy. When I'm hungry, I like to eat. I also love giving advice. It makes me feel smart, appreciated, and valued. The problem is that when you give advice, you are making at least one major mistake. David Marquet, author of *Turn the Ship Around—A True Story of Turning Followers Into Leaders,* once told me that giving advice "robs the other person of an opportunity to think and learn for themselves." Try going an entire day without giving anyone advice. Practice asking questions that help the other person see their challenge from a new perspective.

13. **Don't waste an experience**—There is an old saying, "Adversity is a terrible thing to waste." Completion of a military operation often ends with an after-action report (AAR). Don't wait for some sort of adversity to ask, "What happened?" Make it a habit and commit to AARs. *What was supposed to happen? What actually did happen? What do we think caused the gap in performance? What worked? What contributed most to our success? What didn't work?* Learn from all your projects, not just those that went wrong.

14. **Get curious with yourself**—It's part of the human experience to get angry, embarrassed, frustrated, and anxious. Author and clinical psychologist Susan David recommends that when we're hit with intense, uncomfortable emotions, we ask ourselves, "What is the func?" It's short for "What is the function of this emotion?" We're really asking ourselves, "What is this emotion telling me?" or "Where is it coming from?" We might also ask, "What other emotions may be surfacing?" The basic idea is to pause and reflect. The more we can understand ourselves, the better we are positioned to act in accordance with our most treasured values.

15. **Take a different perspective**—Sometimes, creativity comes from the most unexpected places. Earlier, we talked about the value of getting the perspectives of "rookies." If you don't have access to a rookie brain, consider taking a different point of view. Try asking how a dentist might see this. What might a kindergartener notice about this? What questions might a schoolteacher or waiter ask about this? Not only will you expand your perspective, but you will also build empathy.

16. **When you're stuck, admit it**—Two of the best coaches around, Anne Loehr and Brian Emerson, help teach leaders how to be better coaches. They also believe that a little humility goes a long way when you're trying to ask more questions and express a little more curiosity. If you're not sure what to ask, they recommend

saying, "I'm not sure what to ask you right now ... what do you think I should be asking you?" Your employees will learn that it's okay to say they don't know, and you're helping them think for themselves in the moment. A win-win.

17. **Do something new**—Consider taking on a new responsibility that interests you at work. If you're in customer service, what interests you about sales? How could you help the sales organization set expectations with customers more effectively and reduce churn? If you're in engineering, how might you benefit human resources? What technologies or processes could be used during onboarding to improve the employee experience? It was a move like this (I volunteered to help our internal coaching team) when I worked at Nextel Communications in product development that led to my career in coaching.

18. **Learn something new**—When I was a kid, my parents bought me a subscription to *Sports Illustrated*. I usually read it from cover to cover. It was *naturally* interesting to me. I've since branched out and discovered a desire to learn more about renewable energy, economics, politics, history, and more. If you read a conservative newspaper, consider finding one with a more liberal point of view. If your favorite podcast is all about your favorite football team, try listening to a murder mystery or current events. Just as a good hamstring stretch loosens up your legs and lower back, so does exposing your brain to a diversity of information.

19. **What are we missing?**—You can do this with your team or by yourself. Consider your team's greatest challenge. First ask, "What do we know?" Be careful with this question. Answer only with facts—those things that are proven to be true and cannot be refuted. Next ask, "What do we *think* we know?" Feel free to list your assumptions, stories, beliefs, and conclusions. Pay attention to the differences in the answers to these questions. Finally, ask, "What do we *want* to know?" This should generate a great deal of curiosity for you and your team. It builds permission to have a dialogue and see the gaps between the information you have and that which you need to solve important challenges.

20. **Consider other learning experiences**—Several years ago I thought it might be a good idea to learn a martial art. I settled on jiu-jitsu, the "gentle art"—so called because there is a strong focus on a style of self-defense that attempts to limit harm to an attacker. After several weeks of lessons, I started to think about different scenarios. I imagined what might happen if the guy behind me at Wegmans decided to attack me or how I would get out from under that really big guy at Costco if he got me to the ground. Not all of my curiosity was about self-defense. My brain started to work differently. I was somehow accessing another area that had been untouched for years. It is almost impossible to put it into words—I was more capable of seeing different points of view. I had a new vocabulary and a new way of thinking. It doesn't have to be a martial art. Consider paint-

ing, cooking, yoga, or a host of other activities and hobbies to wake up dormant parts of your brain.

21. **Make a list of great questions**—How did you feel the last time someone said to you, "Wow, that is a great question"? I'm guessing it felt really good. As a coach, I ask questions all day, and whenever I hear a really good question, I add it to a page in Microsoft OneNote. A couple of my favorites:
    - *What am I missing?* (A good question to ask when you're in conflict with someone else.)
    - *How do you see it?* (Open-ended and shows you care what the other person thinks.)
    - *What factors led to that decision?* (Help the other person retrace their steps without getting defensive.)
    - *How is that belief serving your values?* (One of my favorites when you sense other people aren't being true to themselves.)

22. **Listen actively**—Make it a goal to speak less and listen more. This could be in formal one-on-ones, staff meetings, or even informal conversations. Pay attention to the words that people use. Are certain words repeated? Do they seem curious? Do they seem to mix up facts with beliefs, conclusions, stories, and assumptions? In one-on-one conversations, make sure to pause at least 5–7 seconds after someone else has finished speaking. Absorb what they have said and do your best to give them room to continue without interruption.

23. **Argue the opposite**—When you are in conflict with someone else, consider arguing for their side. Ask yourself: *How did they get to this position? What are the merits of their position? What might we have in common? How might their position actually support my ultimate goals? What burden might they be carrying?*

24. **Keep a curiosity journal**—Journaling for short periods (10–20 minutes) over several days at a time has been proven to improve well-being and resilience. Writing allows you to slow down your thinking, and it forces you to organize your thoughts. It can also spark your curiosity. Consider taking notes on the questions and interests that pop into your head over the course of a day. What ideas keep popping up? What questions are going unanswered? What thoughts and feelings seem to have a hold over you? What patterns are you seeing emerge?

25. **Be comfortably uncomfortable**—Of course, we all strive for positive outcomes. We want good health, increased income, and efficient, collaborative teams, for instance. One thing we might desire even more: certainty. As an independent consultant, my income fluctuates from month-to-month and year-to-year. When October rolls around, I start worrying about meeting my financial goals for the following year. It feels a little like coming home from college over Thanksgiving. It's nice to have a break from class and home-

work, although you know you have to get ready for finals when you go back to school. So, imagine what it would be like to replace your worries and anxiety with a little more curiosity. The uncomfortable emotions about the future are natural and can be helpful in smaller doses. Curiosity expands our thinking and takes us down different paths that just might help us come up with more solutions, with the added benefit of improving our well-being.

Pick one or two of these activities and give them a try. Remember to make them your own and email me at info@DRHleadership.com if you have some new ideas!

Chapter 7
What are the risks of having too much curiosity?

"Curiosity killed the cat."—Anonymous

This phrase about the cat is often used as a cautionary proverb for someone who may be seen as overly curious and investigating something that is "none of their business." I'm pretty sure I heard this several times as a child and even as a young adult. While it's not a foolproof way to keep us away from probing into someone else's private affairs, it is a signal between humans that an innocent question is coming across as nosy. In short, curiosity has its downsides just like everything else that is good for us.

Earlier, we shared some of the results of a survey we sponsored on the benefits of curiosity. While curiosity was not ranked highly against other leadership traits, we discovered that competent leaders were seen as highly curious. We also discovered what too much curiosity looked like and what it indicated to survey respondents. Our survey told us that employees see at least five disadvantages.

Being too nosy

Just like the cat who was too curious, we can all let our curiosity get the best of us. Years ago, a friend of mine (we'll call her Jess) had broken up with her boyfriend. I wasn't particularly close to Jess, and I thought it might be nice to ask her some questions and see how she was holding up. What I failed to pay attention to was how she was answering and how uncomfortable she was with my line of questioning. I really wanted to know what happened, how she felt, what this guy was really like, etc. It stopped being about helping her. Now, I was just trying to satisfy my own curiosity. It was selfish.

We live in interesting times. People often have their guard up about personal information at work. There are some who advocate that it's not okay to ask where someone is from anymore. Leaders must exercise caution and think more about how the other person may view their line of questioning than satisfying their own curiosity. Pay attention to how someone answers your questions. What is their body language telling you? How much information are they sharing or guarding?

Asking lots of questions about someone's work might come across as micromanaging.

Indecisiveness

Some employees expect leaders to make decisions. Harry Truman was right when he placed a sign on his desk reading, "The buck stops here." It doesn't mean you can't consult with others. One way to look at decision-making is to put it on a spectrum of involvement. At one end of the spectrum is what we'll refer to as an authoritative style of decision-making. At the other end is collaboration. Both styles have their strengths and weaknesses. And both have their time and place. Neither should be applied in every situation.

Employees want to see progress on the tasks they own, the projects they contribute to, and the decisions that affect their roles. An endless string of questions and inquiry might lead some to believe that you're indecisive. We recommend that you tell your team *why* you are asking questions and gathering multiple points of view. Let them know that you intend to make the final call and you appreciate their input. Again, pay attention to their reactions. Chris Austin (now CEO-Partner of Flagship Pioneering) once told me that one of the most difficult aspects of leading is that the higher you go, the less information you have to make decisions. It's not necessarily fair. It's just reality.

Lack of focus

Over 60% of our survey respondents told us that too much curiosity made them think that their leaders were constantly "chasing the next big idea" and lacking focus on their true priorities. It's a little like going down the rabbit hole on the internet. You hear someone in a meeting mention something about how AI is being used to create deepfakes. So, you Google "deepfakes." Before you know it, you're watching deepfakes and reading articles about how they might be used in politics. Then, you're looking at the latest polls. You stumble upon the most recent polls in New Hampshire. "Wow, I bet New Hampshire is beautiful in the fall," you say to yourself, so you start looking for houses to rent when the foliage is at its peak. And, then you forget why you opened your browser in the first place.

Innately curious people can be amazingly creative exactly because they make connections and go down rabbit holes. It's immensely satisfying, and it scratches an itch. Leaders who practice basic mindfulness catch themselves wandering off target and losing focus.

Lacking confidence and knowledge

When we run workshops for our clients, we do our best to avoid "death by PowerPoint." We design activities that help the participants learn by doing, which may include some individual writing, a conversation with a partner, and large group discussions, to name a few. One thing we try to avoid at all costs is embarrassing a participant with a really difficult question or telling someone that their point of view just doesn't work.

On average, adults hate being embarrassed. Looking incompetent makes some people fear for their jobs. They may not think they will lose their job because of an incoherent answer in a workshop, but when they are paid to deliver as salespeople, marketing managers, supervisors, and accountants, the fear is real. And so it goes with leaders. Being "on stage" every day shines a spotlight on how they respond to questions, how they handle crises, and what they do to solve problems.

Too much curiosity may lead people to think that a manager doesn't have the basic skills and knowledge to do the job. Empathy, connection, self-awareness, humility, and curiosity may be essential to great leadership. So is competence. A thoughtful question that helps the team clarify a problem or rethink how they're approaching an issue is helpful. Asking questions about basics that people expect you to know can hurt your credibility.

Passive-aggressiveness

When I bought my first car, the salesman shuffled me off to their finance manager in a back room to go over the financing and some other paperwork. This person tried to sell me an extended warranty, among other things. He said, "How would you like to pay for the extended warranty?" I was in my early twenties and my mind started to race. *Did I agree to this with the salesperson? Do these cars typically break down before the warranty runs out? Can I afford it? Where is my dad when I need him??!!*

Of course, he wasn't asking me *if* I wanted the extended warranty. He was *persuading* me to make this purchase. It was incredibly uncomfortable and not the type of practice most customers appreciate. Sometimes, as leaders, we ask questions that steer our team in the direction that we want to see them go. Questions like, "Have you thought about going with another vendor?" or "Are you aware that senior leadership is paying very close attention to this project, and they expect it to be completed by the first of the month?"

This sort of curiosity isn't actually curiosity. It is a passive-aggressive attempt to change someone's mind or alter their motivation using questions. Truly curious questions help both the person asking the question and the one receiving the question endeavor to see the situation in a different light and explore options. If you really want a different vendor, make that clear by stating your preference. If you are worried that senior leadership is unhappy with the progress of a key project, say so. Passive-aggressiveness lowers trust, makes conflict worse, has a negative emotional impact on the person receiving it, and it decreases confidence in your leadership.

> **"Curiosity is a willing, a proud, and an eager confession of ignorance."—Unknown**

Luis Viera constantly accesses his humility by reminding himself that he doesn't have all the answers and that this is why he hired a team of really smart people to work with him. He told me, "I adjust to the circumstances." In short, there are times when you will be more directive and times when you will benefit from being curious and collaborative. In the end, Luis says that if you are going to err on one side of this or the other, "Circumstances may change, but don't stop being curious."

It's one thing for a leader to adopt a curious mindset. For curiosity to be a strength of your organization, it's got to become a part of the culture. Next, we'll explore some simple steps you can take to make that so.

Re-Thinking Curiosity

Chapter 8
How can I encourage a culture of curiosity in my organization?

"Culture eats strategy for breakfast."—Peter Drucker

Changing yourself is hard. I work with people every day who are trying to become better leaders. They try new approaches to giving feedback. They attempt to get organized or lead with less micromanaging. Some make more progress than others. The one constant is that I coach one person at a time. It's not easy. It is, however, easier than changing the culture of your organization. But just imagine an army of curious, competent people all moving in the same direction. The goal of this chapter is to share some tips and tricks for driving a little more curiosity into the DNA of your team.

***

Let's start with some research. We've talked about the benefits of curiosity to you as a leader and to you as a human being. What do we know about the value of curiosity to organizations? In short, creating a culture of curiosity is good for business.

Innovation

Asking questions has probably been at the heart of every invention and innovation since the beginning of time. *Why should I have to wait a whole week to send a package across the country?* (FedEx) *Why do I have to send my pictures to someone else to be developed?* (Digital cameras) *What if cars ran on electricity instead of gasoline?* (Tesla) And the list goes on. Asking basic questions that sometimes challenge our basic assumptions leads us to startling answers.

Problem-Solving and Decision-Making

Every day, my clients face new problems, from cutting costs to new competitors to key managers refusing to share information with their peers. The best solutions come from asking questions to *understand* what happened, what the goals are, who is involved, why this might have happened, and how we might approach the challenge in front of us. The best solutions often come from a little bit of patience and a lot of curiosity.

Higher Trust

Consider the last time you lost trust in someone. At some point, you reached a conclusion that this person did not have your best interests in mind, she was not competent, or maybe that she was hiding something. You may have been right.

There may also have been times when the conclusion you came to was wrong and you didn't exercise enough curiosity. Asking just a few questions and aiming for the truth about someone, their motivations, their context, and their skills can help us understand them better. Understanding someone helps you relate to them and communicate more effectively.

Reduced Conflict

I've done some extensive research on conflict (mostly because for the vast majority of my life I avoided it whenever I possibly could). I find it fascinating how this word has a bad rap. If you want to "get good" at disagreeing with others, get curious. Learn how to ask good questions that help both parties think more critically about the subject, because the best way to get someone to change their mind is for them to hear themselves talk.

The best negotiators ask four times as many questions as average negotiators. They also seek agreement. That is, they look for common ground through artful questioning. Now, imagine your organization being an army of great negotiators asking questions to build common ground and attempting to understand each other instead of trying to prove who is "right."

"We run this company on questions, not answers."
—**Eric Schmidt**

Re-Thinking Curiosity

Imagine an army of people being curious about decisions, problems and conflicts. Bias gets replaced with self-awareness and empathy. Problems become opportunities. Conflict leads to innovation.

The case for building a culture of curiosity is a strong one. How exactly do you do it? There are lots of books on this subject and many consulting firms dedicated to doing this right. Below are four thoughts to get you started.

1. Start with "we"

If there is more than one person in your organization, you're going to need engagement, commitment, and input from others to get this right. Your view from the top is important. Your vision and the strategy you set forth are critical for the organization to be successful. As we discussed earlier, if you truly want innovative ideas and you want buy-in from your team, get them involved.

2. Make it a priority

Luis Viera encourages curiosity by tying it to Aleto's core value of ingenuity. Aleto even provides a financial incentive via their "Above and Beyond" program. Luis believes that recognizing valued behavior is so important to their success that there is a financial reward given every quarter.

If you believe that "culture eats strategy for breakfast" as Luis does, then make this a priority. Don't just delegate this to a couple of enthusiasts on your team who do some research, put a PowerPoint together, and present it at the next all-hands meeting. Don't think that hiring a culture expert and asking her to speak for an hour at your next off-site will get the job done, either.

If it's truly important to you, commit to it and stay involved. Ask for updates. Participate in discussions. Early on, determine your role, deadlines, deliverables, and outcomes. In short, treat it like any other important project. Recognize that building the foundation will take months, at a minimum. Realizing a healthy, strong culture can take years. It's well worth the effort and wait.

3. Don't be a hypocrite

I was first introduced to Steve Wiley in 2019 by a mutual colleague. Steve is experienced, smart, and has a heart the size of North Carolina, which is where his wife and kids call home. Being a curious, humble person, Steve started our initial conversation by asking me to share a little bit about myself and my business.

Re-Thinking Curiosity

I told him that most of my business was focused on coaching executives, and I still facilitated corporate training and leadership team building and off-sites. Pretty basic stuff in our profession.

I reciprocated with a similar question, and Steve responded with another question. "Doug, you know how your clients have a strategic plan, an IT roadmap, and even a marketing plan?" he asked. "Yup," I said, and he responded with, "Do any of them have a culture plan?" I was hooked just by his question. An actual plan to manage your culture? Brilliant! I'd never heard of a culture plan, and I couldn't wait to hear about it. Steve's firm, CEEK (you can check them out at www.CEEKLLC.com), helps companies implement an "intentional culture" from start to finish.

If you're like me, you're a little skeptical of the real impact of having a vision, mission, and stated values. Efforts to articulate these high-minded elements of culture often start off with enthusiasm and are quickly overshadowed by the day's priority. Mission, vision, and values have been discussed so much that efforts to develop them are often met with skepticism. *Is this really worth our time?* CEEK helps companies overcome the skepticism and the lack of prioritization by administering a "hypocrisy index." In short, they customize a unique survey that gives employees the chance to evaluate the mission, vision, and values while also stating whether their leaders are behaving in ways that are consistent with these proclamations. What good is it to state, for instance, that "collaboration" is a core value when there is a dictatorial style of leadership and the organization's leaders seem to be competing with each other? Steve and his team sometimes come across leaders that want to pay his team to help them build the plan, but they're not so eager to see where they fall on the hypocrisy index. Leaders who practice humility and curiosity get the opportunity to build trust by saying, "We hear you. We're going to change the way we behave."

4. Listen and learn (from several great leaders)

In the introduction, I talked about my dad reading and highlighting books. I thought it was cool to be curious and learn. I wanted to be more like my dad. In the early 1960s, psychologist Albert Bandura ran a series of experiments with children to test his "social learning theory." In short, Bandura held that new behaviors are typically acquired by observing and imitating others.

The experiments were fairly simple. An adult sat in one corner of the room with an inflatable "Bobo" doll, which had a heavy base so when someone pushed it or punched it, the doll would return to its upright position. In the other corner of the room was a child. The child had several small items to play with for several minutes.

In one condition, the adult showed aggressive behavior toward the doll by hitting it with a mallet, punching it with their fist, or yelling at it in anger. In the second condition, the adult ignored the doll and played with other toys. In both cases, the adult left the room after ten minutes and the experimenter brought the child to another room, telling the child that they could play with the toys in the new room. After two minutes, the child was told that they could no longer play with the toys in that room with the goal of building frustration in the child. Then the child was brought back to the original room and observed. Children who were exposed to the "aggressive" adult were more likely to follow this lead and be aggressive toward the doll.

Adults also model the behaviors of those they respect. This is why I believe Steve Wiley's hypocrisy index is so valuable. Don't ask your employees to be curious, then ridicule them for a poorly timed question. Don't ask them to be innovative, then mock a wild suggestion. One leadership team I witnessed had notepads distributed to employees with the following printed on every page, "Act like an owner." The goal was to get employees thinking more about cutting costs, but it fell on deaf ears when the leaders of the firm were flying first class and ordering expensive desk chairs. So, be nice to the Bobo doll. Be like Michael Chiock.

Michael, Partner and Managing Director at AlixPartners, was recently given feedback that he encourages all his team members to ask questions and be curious. He does two simple things that just about any leader can do. First, model being curious. As you read earlier, Michael is constantly reading, asking questions, and genuinely being curious about the world, his colleagues, his industry, and his clients. It comes from a place of humility and openness. Employees see this. They can feel it. *If Michael can say, "Hmmm ... I don't know. What do you think?" it must be okay for me to be curious.*

Once you model curiosity in all its forms, you get to see others follow suit. This is where the second principle must take hold. In 2012, Google initiated an internal study with the goal of determining what made some of their teams successful and why others failed to live up to their potential. What they found surprised them. The number one factor was whether the members of the team felt "psychologically safe." That is, team members were able to share their facts, opinions, beliefs, assumptions, and conclusions without fear of being ridiculed or punished in any way. They also felt safe asking questions. Again, adults are not usually quick to put their ignorance on display. Like the best Google managers, Michael Chiock's team is encouraged to ask questions. "Dumb" questions are not derided. When someone asks a "bad" question, consider it a gift. This person is being genuinely vulnerable. It's an opportunity for you to be patient, inquisitive, and maybe even recognize that this person needs further coaching or training. Michael's goal is to "listen intently to understand." While he may not accept the premise of the question or even the argument being put forth, he makes sure to provide the rationale for his position to keep it "safe." If the questions stop coming, then everyone stops learning and growing.

When I asked an executive at a government agency for some advice about building a culture of curiosity, she was almost embarrassed because she had nothing "innovative" (her word, not mine!) to offer. I wasn't necessarily searching for innovative. I wanted to know what worked. I said, "Let's hear it." "Well," she replied, "I've made a commitment to always ask questions and talk less." That's it. And that's great!

While some may hire consultants and put together committees to create an intentional culture, this executive's advice is more than sound for smaller teams. Remember, as a leader, you are on stage every day, as noted by Marcus Buckingham and Curt Coffman, authors of *First Break All The Rules—What the World's Greatest Managers Do Differently*. Your employees remember what you wore yesterday, how you greeted them this morning, and when you interrupted them in this afternoon's staff meeting. The lights are bright on this stage, and your team has front-row seats. If they see you being curious, it's a good bet they'll follow suit.

Bill Staffieri, a Partner at PwC, offers similar advice: "I share examples of the benefits of asking questions. Those examples could be related to asking more questions to get to know someone better and building stronger, more meaningful relationships, or they could be related to specific work areas that they are tasked with on a particular engagement. I emphasize the importance of asking questions and being curious with everything that they approach—both personally and professionally. I tell them that without curiosity and asking questions, they may never fully understand or appreciate something, especially since none of us know everything."

Gail Fisher's time in the military (33 years) taught her some valuable lessons. She started out as a private working as a mechanic and ended up as a Civil Affairs officer doing strategy work on the Joint Staff. Gail retired in August of 2021 with the rank of full Colonel. Along the way, she served under some "brilliant" leaders and she suffered under a number of incompetent ones, as well. Being a curious person, she learned from both types of leaders.

Gail discovered that she didn't really like the idea of telling people what to do, and she knew that some just needed a little nudge in place of a direct order. One of her favorite tactics was what I refer to as "plant the seed." When having a conversation with someone in her unit about their career or a problem they were trying to solve, Gail resisted telling them what to do. She asked some tough questions to help them examine the situation, then she backed off. "Well," she would say, "I'm gonna leave this one to you! Can you think about all this and then let's talk some more in a week?" Some people need time to think. They need to go away and ponder deeper questions. If you have someone like this on your team, consider Gail's advice and lead people through a problem, but let them solve it.

Whatever your approach to culture, be intentional. Model what you want to see in your organization and make it a priority. Few things are as powerful as an organization or team with a strong culture that supports people asking questions, challenging the status quo, and learning. Curiosity just may be the best weapon in the fight against what Steve Wiley calls the "army of zombies"— an organization where people just go through the motions and collect a paycheck. They do the minimum.

Emphasizing and supporting curiosity gives people purpose … every day. *How can I make a difference? What do our customers really want from us? How do we improve our processes?* If you believe curiosity will make you a better leader (and I hope you do!), consider spreading the wealth and making it a core value of your team and organization.

Re-Thinking Curiosity

Conclusion

> "You could fill two internets with what
> I don't know about football."—Ted Lasso

Authors often try to convince you that their idea is the greatest thing since sliced bread. Their interviews, research, and anecdotes all paint a dramatic picture of greater achievement if you will just follow their advice. To some extent, this author is guilty as charged. I tried to mitigate some of the hubris with chapter 7 *(What are the risks of having too much curiosity?)*, but I'm not sure I succeeded. In the end, I am convinced that a dose of humility enables your curiosity, which can then take your leadership to new heights.

I will admit that curiosity is not the cure-all for leaders. Decisiveness, experience, creativity, and raw intelligence (among other characteristics) all play a role in the success of leaders and their organizations. Decisiveness is critical for roles that require accelerated decision-making. Experience is a must in industries where knowledge is key. Raw intelligence allows a leader to understand complex challenges and solve difficult problems.

Simply being curious does not make one a great leader. But lacking curiosity almost assuredly **prevents** one from being great. Curiosity (much like humility) is a nutrient for almost all other leadership characteristics. It enhances them and allows for growth in these areas. The curious *and* decisive leader asks, "Do I really need to decide right now? How might consulting with my team improve this decision?" The curious *and* experienced CEO wonders, "What mistakes have I made that could guide me now? How is my experience creating blind spots for me?" The curious *and* creative manager asks, "How might we find a new way to approach this old problem? Who else can offer some suggestions to solve this problem?" The curious *and* intelligent executive asks, "How might I be wrong? What are we missing in this situation?"

Aside from life-and-death situations that require intuitive, quick decisions and actions-based extensive training (think leaders in military combat and first responders), what is the risk of being curious even if only for a few minutes? We began this journey talking about how the best leadership coaches ask the "right" questions at the "right" times to help their clients figure things out. And while I'm biased about leading with curiosity, it's difficult for me to think of situations where some level of curiosity is actually a bad thing. Pausing, just for a moment, and asking yourself and others a couple of powerful, open-ended questions just might save the day.

I wrote this book *for* leaders. I wrote it for you. Guiding, mentoring, challenging, deciding, solving, and managing are all difficult. They are more difficult in today's economic and social climate. Many leaders are stressed and pulled in too many directions. I see it every day as a coach. My hope is that by bringing just a little more curiosity to your role, you will recognize that you don't have to guide, mentor, challenge, decide, solve, and manage all by yourself. Asking questions and fostering a curious culture brings more intelligent minds to bear. David Marquet said it eloquently, "You have been genetically and culturally programmed to take charge and make it happen, take control and attract followers. What you want is to *give* control and *create* leaders."

Sumeet Sabharwal takes curiosity seriously. I could feel his enthusiasm when I asked him about curiosity and culture. "It's a great question you pose, and before I dive into it, I want to set the stage for how I view curiosity," he shared. "If you had asked me this question a few years ago, I would have viewed it in the limited context of intellectual curiosity that propels growth—both for self and others around. The act of probing deeper to gain a fuller perspective on a topic or subject that I may have limited knowledge of. While that is still a key aspect, there is a second one around openness—more specifically opening our minds to new possibilities and getting past the prejudices we may hold. As we work through complex decisions or I run into team members that may have entrenched opinions that differ from mine, I increasingly find myself slowing down, allowing both the time and the space to listen with intention and an open mind, probing deeper, and exercising the curiosity muscle as part of a genuine desire to bridge the gap."

Curiosity is that bridge for leaders. Whether you are scratching an itch or directing your attention to a priority, curiosity is a vital force that invites continuous learning and growth. It encourages leaders to venture beyond the known and explore new ideas. It fosters a mindset of inquiry and openness and elevates the leader to become an architect of innovation and progress. As leaders tread this bridge, they not only close the gap between what is and what could be but also inspire their teams to embark on the journey with them, building a culture where curiosity is celebrated, and knowledge is continually expanded.

Acknowledgments

There are so many people to thank for help making this book a reality. In my usual way, I started to create a spreadsheet to make sure that I thanked all the right people from all the different steps in the process (research, writing, editing, creative, etc.) and all the different areas of my life (friends, family, clients, colleagues, etc.). It was at this point that I realized everyone mentioned below falls into "friends and family." I am eternally grateful to each person listed and I fully understand that even though there is only one name on the cover, everyone should be getting the credit.

My amazing, curious, empathic, caring wife Tammy Hensch listened to me talk about the concepts in here endlessly. Her encouragement and contributions (she may be the best leader I've ever met!) to this effort leave me speechless.

My best friend and 'brother from another mother,' Jim Hock, read every word (and critiqued every other word) in this book… and made it twice as good. Always willing to help. Always willing to talk. Always willing to advise.

If you actually read the first two chapters, you would know that my unquenchable thirst for knowledge, tools, answers and more questions comes from the two best parents a person could have. Rich and Joyce Hensch are the number one reason for my success and happiness. They fed my curiosity and always supported me in every way. And they continue to do so.

Re-Thinking Curiosity

I am proud to say that Nicholas Hensch's first business experience came with my company, The DRH Group. Among other things, Nick read the first draft of the manuscript and provided edits that I could only dream of when I was a sophomore in college. More than that, he has already recognized the value of curiosity in leadership and life. I want to be more like Nick.

Zach Hensch may not have reviewed any chapters (he was very, very busy pledging a fraternity and acclimating to college life), but he listened to my ideas. He gave me his approval on the book cover and he has listened (OK, pretended to listen) to my talking about curiosity since he was in diapers.

We've all heard, "Don't judge a book by its cover." I'd be thrilled if readers did just that! Sissy Estes (once again) has designed a cover that captures the essence of two concepts (curiosity and leadership) that are not easy to represent in an interesting, appealing way. In addition, Sissy designed a specific graphic for each chapter to help bring the printed words to life.

Once again, Bethany Kelly and her team at Publishing Partner helped me realize that there really is no such thing as "independent publishing." It takes a team to produce a quality book. This is a poorly-written, half-finished Word document without her and her team's expertise and patience.

Who needs an editor? Every one of us! I wish we could clone Frank Steele. It's one thing to provide edits that make a book better. It's another thing to provide edits in a way that make the author better and do so with compassion. Frank is indispensable.

Speaking of indispensable, Dan Porter and Jeff Akin are amazing friends who understand what good writing looks like and how difficult it can be to get a book published. Both Dan and Jeff were constant sources of encouragement.

Max Wiley helped me conduct and interpret a survey that was a first for me. He helped me think through the idea of looking for 'flavors' of curiosity. A captain of the men's soccer team at The College of Wooster (in only his junior year!), Max can easily teach us all a thing or two about leadership!

It's easy to see why Max is such a smart, humble and effective leader when you meet his dad, Steve Wiley. Even though Steve played on the wrong side of the ball in college (he was a defensive back at William & Mary), I learn something every time we talk.

Last and not least, I am eternally grateful to the extraordinary leaders who sat for interviews and answered multiple emails to make this book relevant with real-life examples. Thank you Admiral John Richardson, Chris Austin, Michael Chiock, Gail Fisher, Kiera McCaffrey, Sumeet Sabharwal, Bill Staffieri, Luis Viera, Katherine Huh and Barry Coleman.

Re-Thinking Curiosity

Sources

Chapter 1—Why is leading others so difficult?

Austin, Robert D., and Gary P. Pisano. "Neurodiversity as a Competitive Advantage." *Harvard Business Review* (magazine), May–June 2017. https://hbr.org/2017/05/neurodiversity-as-a-competitive-advantage

Gallup. "What Is Employee Engagement and How Do You Improve It?" Accessed September 15, 2023. https://www.gallup.com/workplace/285674/improve-employee-engagement-workplace.aspx?utm_source=google&utm_medium=cpc&utm_campaign=gallup_access_branded&utm_term=gallup%20employee%20engagement&gclid=CjwKCAjw6p-oBhAYEiwAgg2PgtlRXWpOFwDkgvvO-QD1QK5rE7FUF_BYDpWYucm_WpUgTzyxkRPjBQxoCMYcQAvD_BwE

Grant, Adam. "Daniel Kahneman Doesn't Trust Your Intuition—ReThinking with Adam Grant." TED Audio Collective, January 12, 2023, 36:01. https://www.youtube.com/watch?v=LT40PZyXWyg

Grivas, Chris, and Gerard Puccio. *The Innovative Team: Unleashing Creative Potential for Breakthrough Results.* John Wiley & Sons, 2011.

Hunt, Vivian, Lareina Yee, Sara Prince, and Sundiatu Dixon-Fyle. "Delivering Through Diversity." McKinsey & Company, January 18, 2018. https://www.mckinsey.com/capabilities/people-and-organizational-performance/our-insights/delivering-through-diversity

Leslie, Ian. *Curious: The Desire to Know and Why Your Future Depends On It*. Basic Books, 2015.

Lorenzo, Rocio, and Martin Reeves. "How and Where Diversity Drives Financial Performance." *Harvard Business Review*, January 30, 2018. https://hbr.org/2018/01/how-and-where-diversity-drives-financial-performance#:~:text=Summary,to%20examine%20the%20relationship%20between

Lowney, Declan, dir. *Ted Lasso*. Season 3, episode 12, "So Long, Farewell." Aired May 31, 2023, on Apple TV+.

Michaels, Ed, Helen Handfield-Jones, and Beth Axelrod. *The War for Talent*. Harvard Business Press, 2001.

Turban, Stephen, Dan Wu, and Letian (LT) Zhang. "Research: When Gender Diversity Makes Firms More Productive." *Harvard Business Review*, February 11, 2019. https://hbr.org/2019/02/research-when-gender-diversity-makes-firms-more-productive#:~:text=In%20a%20recent%20study%20of,measured%20by%20market%20value%20and

Turkle, Sherry. *Reclaiming Conversation: The Power of Talk in a Digital Age*. Penguin, 2016.

Wiseman, Liz. "Rookie Smarts: Why Learning Beats Knowing in the New Game of Work." *Leader to Leader* 2015, no. 76 (2015): 54–59.

Chapter 2—Why doesn't the old way work?

Catmull, Ed, and Amy Wallace. *Creativity, Inc. (The Expanded Edition): Overcoming the Unseen Forces That Stand in the Way of True Inspiration*. Random House, 2014.

Deci, Edward L., and Richard Flaste. *Why We Do What We Do: Understanding Self-Motivation*. Penguin, 1996.

Fisher, Gail (President and Colonel, retired). Interview by Doug Hensch, May 30, 2023.

Fredrickson, Barbara L. *Love 2.0: Creating Happiness and Health in Moments of Connection*. Penguin, 2013.

Isaacson, Walter. *Steve Jobs*. Simon and Schuster, 2011.

Kashdan, Todd. *Curious? Discover the Missing Ingredient to a Fulfilling Life*. William Morrow & Co, 2009.

Lashinsky, Adam. *Inside Apple: How America's Most Admired—and Secretive—Company Really Works*. Hachette UK, 2012.

"Leadership Survey for Employees." Conducted through SurveyMonkey, December 14, 2022.

Livio, Mario. *Why?: What Makes Us Curious*. Simon and Schuster, 2017.

Lukianoff, Greg, and Jonathan Haidt. *The Coddling of the American Mind: How Good Intentions and Bad Ideas Are Setting Up a Generation for Failure*. Penguin, 2019.

Marquet, L. David. *Turn the Ship Around!: A True Story of Turning Followers into Leaders*. Penguin, 2013.

MindSpring. "MindSpring Presents: 'Greatness' by David Marquet." October 8, 2013. 9:40. https://www.youtube.com/watch?v=OqmdLcyES_Q&t=3s

Pink, Daniel H. *Drive: The Surprising Truth About What Motivates Us*. Penguin, 2011.

"Pity the modern manager—burnt-out, distracted and overloaded." *Economist*, October 24, 2023. https://www.economist.com/business/2023/10/24/pity-the-modern-manager-burnt-out-distracted-and-overloaded

Porter, Michael E., and Nitin Nohria. "How CEOs Manage Time." *Harvard Business Review* (magazine), July–August 2018. https://hbr.

org/2018/07/how-ceos-manage-time#:~:text=Altogether%2C%20 the%20CEOs%20in%20our,of%2062.5%20hours%20a%20week

Stanier, Michael Bungay. *The Advice Trap: Be Humble, Stay Curious & Change the Way You Lead Forever.* Page Two Books, 2020.

Twenge, Jean M., and W. Keith Campbell. *The Narcissism Epidemic: Living in the Age of Entitlement.* Simon and Schuster, 2009.

Valerio, Joe (Chief Operating Officer). Interview by Doug Hensch, February 5, 2024.

Chapter 3—What is the solution?

Bogart, Julie. *Raising Critical Thinkers: A Parent's Guide to Growing Wise Kids in the Digital Age.* Perigee Books, 2023

Kashdan, Todd. *Curious? Discover the Missing Ingredient to a Fulfilling Life.* William Morrow & Co, 2009.

"Leadership Survey for Employees." Conducted through SurveyMonkey, December 14, 2022.

Livio, Mario. *Why?: What Makes Us Curious.* Simon and Schuster, 2017.

Mandel, David, dir. *The White House Plumbers* (miniseries). Premiered on HBO May 1, 2023. *The White House Plumbers* podcast series also premiered May 1, 2023, available at https://podcasts.apple.com/us/podcast/white-house-plumbers-podcast/id1682542231

Porter, Michael E., and Nitin Nohria. "How CEOs Manage Time." *Harvard Business Review* (magazine), July–August 2018. https://hbr.org/2018/07/how-ceos-manage-time#:~:text=Altogether%2C%20 the%20CEOs%20in%20our,of%2062.5%20hours%20a%20week

VIA Institute on Character. "Curiosity." Accessed August 22, 2023. https://viacharacter.org/character-strengths/curiosity

Chapter 4—What makes curiosity so important?

Anderson, Craig L., Dante D. Dixson, Maria Monroy, and Dacher Keltner. "Are awe-prone people more curious? The relationship between dispositional awe, curiosity, and academic outcomes." *Journal of Personality* 88, no. 4 (August 2020): 762–779. https://doi.org/10.1111/jopy.12524.

Austin, Christopher (CEO-Partner). Interview by Doug Hensch, January 23, 2023.

Blanchard, Tamar, Robert E. McGrath, and Eranda Jayawickreme. "Resilience in the face of interpersonal loss: The role of character strengths." *Applied Psychology: Health and Well-Being* 13, no. 4 (November 2021): 817–834. https://doi.org/10.1111/aphw.12273

Brainy Quote. "Friedrich Nietzsche Quotes." Accessed on December 15, 2023. https://www.brainyquote.com/authors/friedrich-nietzsche-quotes

Chiock, Michael (Partner & Managing Director). Interview by Doug Hensch, May 30, 2023.

David, Susan. *Emotional Agility: Get Unstuck, Embrace Change, and Thrive in Work and Life*. Penguin, 2016.

Hidden Brain Media. "Healing 2.0: What We Gain From Pain." Podcast, 53:40. Accessed December 20, 2023. https://hiddenbrain.org/podcast/what-we-gain-from-pain/

Macaskill, Ann, and Andrew Denovan. "Assessing psychological health: The contribution of psychological strengths." *British Journal of Guidance & Counselling* 42, no. 3 (2014): 320–337. http://dx.doi.org/10.1080/03069885.2014.898739

Proyer, René, Fabian Gander, Sara Wellenzohn, and Willibald Ruch. "What good are character strengths beyond subjective well-being? The contribution of the good character on self-reported health-oriented behavior, physical fitness, and the subjective health status." *Journal of Positive Psychology* 8, no. 3 (May 2013): 222–232. https://doi.org/10.1080/17439760.2013.777767

Vasileiou, Dimitra, Despina Moraitou, Vasileios Papaliagkas, Christos Pezirkianidis, Anastasios Stalikas, Georgia Papantoniou, and Maria Sofologi. "The Relationships between Character Strengths and Subjective Wellbeing: Evidence from Greece under Lockdown during COVID-19 Pandemic." *International Journal of Environmental Research and Public Health* 18, no. 20 (October 2021): 10868. https://www.mdpi.com/1660-4601/18/20/10868

Chapter 5—Who can show me the way?

Huh, Katherine (Partner). Interview by Doug Hensch, June 6, 2023.

McCaffrey, Kiera (Principal). Interview by Doug Hensch, May 31, 2023.

Richardson, John (Chief of Naval Operations, US Navy, retired). Interview by Doug Hensch, May 23, 2023.

Sabharwal, Sumeet (Chief Executive Officer). Interview by Doug Hensch, May 31, 2023.

U.S. Department of Defense. "John M. Richardson." Accessed December 7, 2023. https://www.defense.gov/About/Biographies/Biography/Article/621885/admiral-john-m-richardson-retired/

Viera, Luis (President). Interview by Doug Hensch, June 29, 2023.

Chapter 6—What else can I do?

Benson, Kyle. "How Being Nuanced with Your Emotions Enhances Your Well-Being: An Interview with Susan David, Ph.D., Part II." The Gottman Institute. Accessed October 22, 2023. https://www.gottman.com/blog/how-being-nuanced-with-your-emotions-enhances-your-well-being-an-interview-with-susan-david-ph-d-part-ii/

Berger, Warren. *A More Beautiful Question: The Power of Inquiry to Spark Breakthrough Ideas*. Bloomsbury USA, 2014.

Boudreau, Emily. "A Curious Mind." Harvard Graduate School of Education, November 24, 2020. https://www.gse.harvard.edu/ideas/usable-knowledge/20/11/curious-mind

David, Susan. *Emotional Agility: Get Unstuck, Embrace Change, and Thrive in Work and Life*. Penguin, 2016.

Dweck, Carol S. *Mindset: The New Psychology of Success*. Random House, 2006.

Loehr, Anne, and Brian Emerson. *A Manager's Guide to Coaching: Simple and Effective Ways to Get the Best From Your Employees*. AMACOM, 2008.

Pennebaker, James W. *Opening Up: The Healing Power of Expressing Emotions*. Guilford Press, 2012.

Robinson, Alan G., and Dean M. Schroeder. *The Idea-Driven Organization: Unlocking the Power in Bottom-Up Ideas*. Berrett-Koehler Publishers, 2020.

Schein, Edgar H., and Peter A. Schein. *Humble Inquiry: The Gentle Art of Asking Instead of Telling*. Berrett-Koehler Publishers, 2021.

Stanier, Michael Bungay. *The Advice Trap: Be Humble, Stay Curious & Change the Way You Lead Forever*. Page Two Books, 2020.

Turkle, Sherry. *Reclaiming Conversation: The Power of Talk in a Digital Age*. Penguin, 2016.

Yoon, Jaewon, Hayley Blunden, Ariella Kristal, and Ashley Whillans. "Why Asking for Advice Is More Effective Than Asking For Feedback." *Harvard Business Review*, September 20, 2019. https://hbr.org/2019/09/why-asking-for-advice-is-more-effective-than-asking-for-feedback

Chapter 7—What are the risks of having too much curiosity?

Austin, Christopher (CEO-Partner). Interview by Doug Hensch, January 23, 2023.

"Leadership Survey for Employees." Conducted through SurveyMonkey, December 14, 2022.

Pinker, Steven. "A five-point plan to save Harvard from itself." *The Boston Globe*, December 11, 2023. https://www.bostonglobe.com/2023/12/11/opinion/steven-pinker-how-to-save-universities-harvard-claudine-gay/

Viera, Luis (President). Interview by Doug Hensch, June 29, 2023.

Chapter 8— How can I encourage a culture of curiosity in my organization?

Bandura, Albert. *The Praeger Handbook of Education and Psychology* [4 volumes]. Edited by Joe L. Kincheloe and Raymond A. Horn Jr. Praeger, 2006, 49.

Buckingham, Marcus, and Curt Coffman. *First, Break All the Rules: What the World's Greatest Managers Do Differently*. Simon and Schuster, 2014.

Casanova, Carlos. "Google Project Aristotle—5 Keys to Team Success." Tech Target Network, September 14, 2016. https://www.techtarget.

com/searchitoperations/blog/Modern-Operations-Apps-Stacks/
   Google-Project-Aristotle-5-Keys-to-Team-Success
Chiock, Michael (Partner and Managing Director). Interview by Doug Hensch, May 30, 2023.
Fisher, Gail (President and Colonel, retired). Interview by Doug Hensch, May 30, 2023.
Gino, Francesca. "The Business Case for Curiosity." *Harvard Business Review* (magazine), September–October 2018. https://hbr.org/2018/09/the-business-case-for-curiosity?ab=seriesnav-spotlight
Grant, Adam. *Think Again: The Power of Knowing What You Don't Know*. Penguin, 2023.
"Leadership Survey for Employees." Conducted through SurveyMonkey, December 14, 2022.
McRaney, David. *How Minds Change: The Surprising Science of Belief, Opinion, and Persuasion*. Penguin, 2022.
Miller, William R., and Stephen Rollnick. *Motivational Interviewing: Helping People Change*. Guilford Press, 2012.
Sharot, Tali. *The Influential Mind: What the Brain Reveals About Our Power to Change Others*. Henry Holt and Company, 2017.
Staffieri, Bill (Partner). Interview by Doug Hensch, June 1, 2023.
Viera, Luis (President). Interview by Doug Hensch, June 29, 2023.

Conclusion

Marshall, Tom, dir. *Ted Lasso*. Season 1, episode 1, "Pilot." Aired August 14, 2020, on Apple TV+.
Sabharwal, Sumeet (Chief Executive Officer). Interview by Doug Hensch, May 31, 2023.

Re-Thinking Curiosity